Canoeing and Kayaking BC's Central Interior:

A Guidebook [sixth edition]

Edited by: Wayne Giles and Barbara Robertson

Published by:

Northwest Brigade Paddling Club

Prince George, British Columbia

Front cover photo credits: canoeist, Marian Tamkin
kayaker, Dallas Eng

Back cover photo credits: top of page kayaker, Ed Day
man and dog, Wayne Giles
kayaker, one of Al's pals
canoeists, Wayne Giles

Published by:

Northwest Brigade Paddling Club

P.O. Box 327

Prince George, British Columbia

V2L 4S2

Printed in Canada

Cover design: Peter Maides

Index: Kathy Plett

National Library of Canada Cataloguing in Publication Data

Main entry under title:

Canoeing and kayaking BC's Central Interior

Includes index.
ISBN 0-9731224-0-4

1. Canoes and canoeing--British Columbia. 2. Kayaking--British Columbia. 3. British Columbia--Guidebooks. I. Giles, Wayne, date II. Robertson, Barbara, date III. Northwest Brigade Paddling Club.

GV776.15.B7C35 2002 797.1'22'097117 C2001-902490-8

Table of Contents

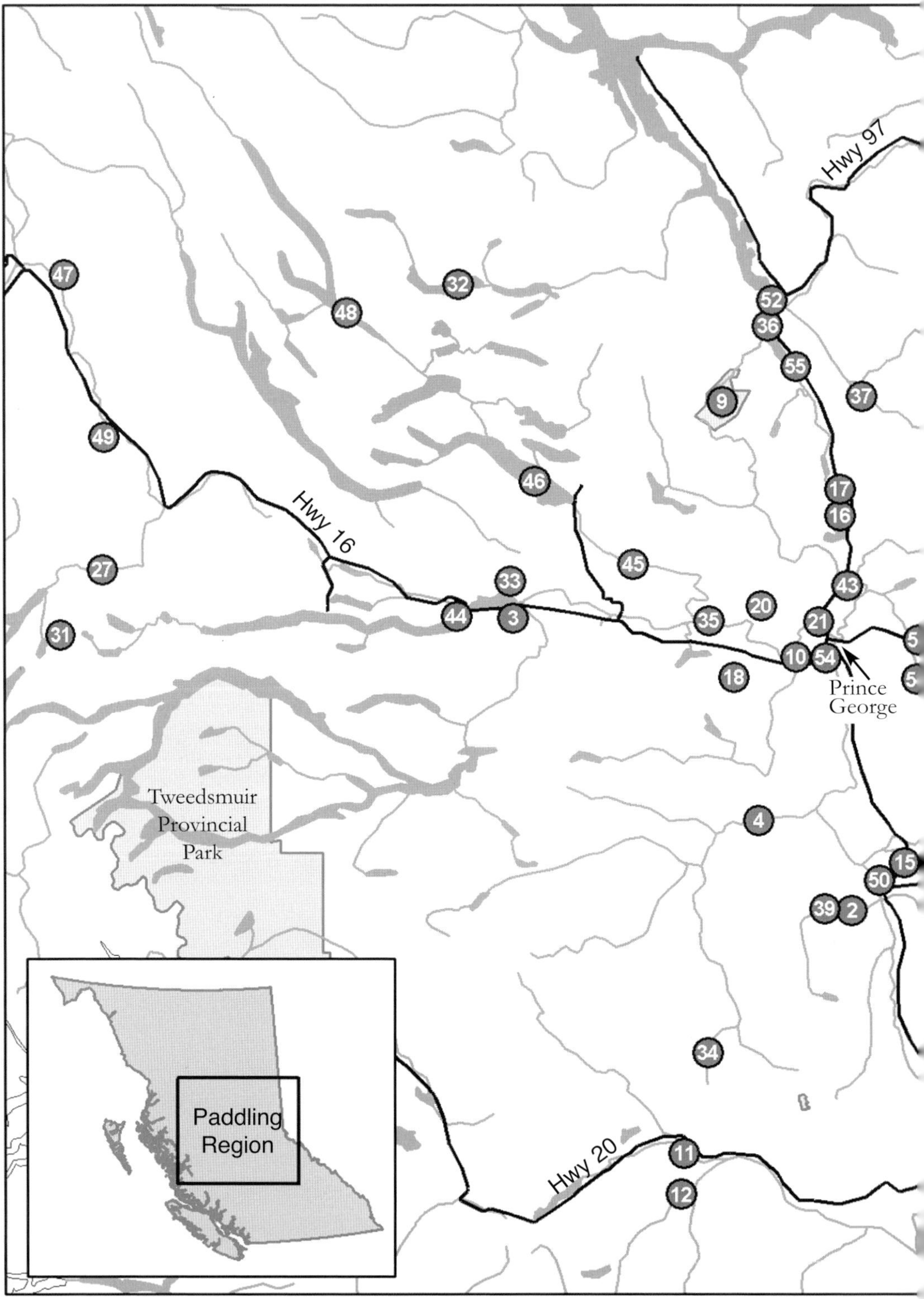
Hwy 97
Hwy 16
Hwy 20
Prince George
Tweedsmuir Provincial Park
Paddling Region
47
48
32
52
36
55
9
37
49
46
17
16
45
27
33
43
20
44
3
35
21
31
10
54
18
4
15
50
39
2
34
11
12

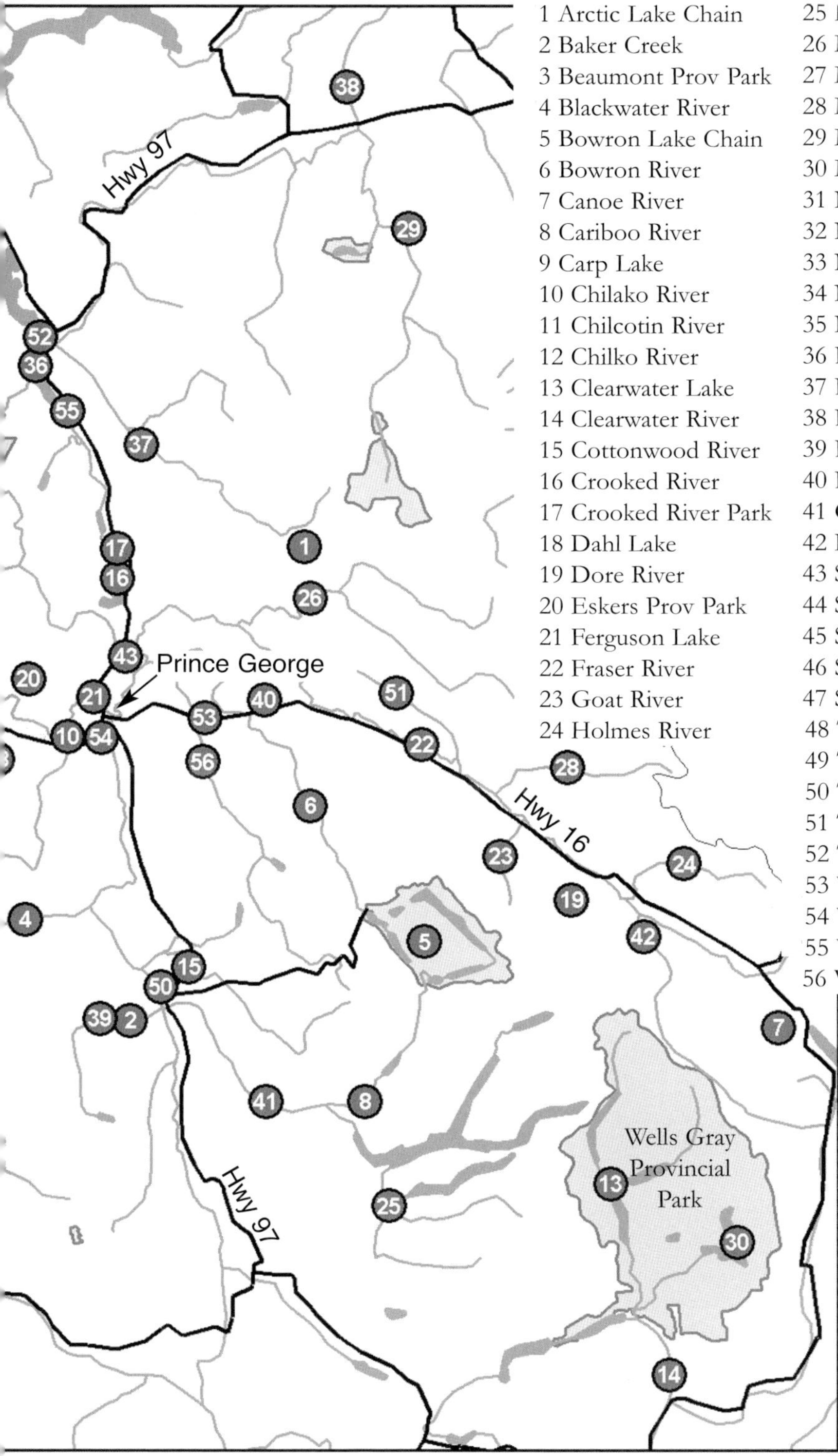

1 Arctic Lake Chain
2 Baker Creek
3 Beaumont Prov Park
4 Blackwater River
5 Bowron Lake Chain
6 Bowron River
7 Canoe River
8 Cariboo River
9 Carp Lake
10 Chilako River
11 Chilcotin River
12 Chilko River
13 Clearwater Lake
14 Clearwater River
15 Cottonwood River
16 Crooked River
17 Crooked River Park
18 Dahl Lake
19 Dore River
20 Eskers Prov Park
21 Ferguson Lake
22 Fraser River
23 Goat River
24 Holmes River
25 Horsefly River
26 McGregor River
27 Morice River
28 Morkill River
29 Murray River
30 Murtle Lake
31 Nanika Lake Chain
32 Nation Lake Chain
33 Nautley River
34 Nazko Lake Chain
35 Nechako River
36 Pack River
37 Parsnip River
38 Pine River
39 Puntchesakut Lake
40 Purden Lake
41 Quesnel River
42 Raush River
43 Salmon River
44 Stellako River
45 Stuart Lake Parks
46 Stuart River
47 Suskwa River
48 Takla Landing
49 Telkwa River
50 Ten-Mile Lake Park
51 Torpy River
52 Tudyah Lake Park
53 Wansa Creek
54 West Lake
55 Whiskers Point Park
56 Willow River

Disclaimer

The editors, authors, publisher, and contributors to this book hereby disclaim all liability for injury, death, property damage, or any other harm, loss, or damage, caused, or alleged to be caused, directly or indirectly by the information contained in this book.

This book contains general information only, collected over many years by many volunteers. River, road and environmental conditions constantly change. Therefore, we do not guarantee the accuracy or currency of any information contained in this book.

This book is no substitute for the knowledge, skills, and experience required for a safe trip. The reader must evaluate his or her own skills and the present conditions and obtain appropriate instruction and additional information before undertaking any trip.

Preface

Paddling opportunities in BC's Central Interior are plentiful. From the towns of Clearwater to Mackenzie and Jasper to Smithers the region offers a variety of paddling from Interior Plateau extended flatwater trips to short whitewater playboating through mountain scenery. The superb paddling in this area is little known beyond local communities. The Northwest Brigade Paddling Club has developed many programs over the years that have equipped paddlers with the skills and knowledge to explore our waterways. We hope this book helps to encourage more people to experience the world class paddling that abounds in this diverse landscape.

This guidebook does not cover all the potential trips in the area. There are many rivers yet to be explored and countless lakes not mentioned here, that are already well-known favorites. For this guide we chose to feature only those lakes that are within parks or that are part of longer wilderness trips. And we've even missed some of these!

Members of the Northwest Brigade Paddling Club have shared their paddling experiences with others starting with the first edition of the club guide book in 1980. Though this book has evolved and in this edition includes a name change, the contributors range back through the history of the club. The editors, in an effort to achieve consistency of style, have altered trip descriptions. We hope the descriptions herein still convey the true nature of the trip intended by the authors.

Happy paddling.

Acknowledgements

We would like to thank the following people for their help with the preparation of this book. Without their contributions of trip reports, stories and pictures this book would be a great deal thinner! In addition, thank you to those who put much time and effort into compiling and contributing to the previous editions of this book.

Ed Day, Paul Walsh, Ian Norn, Greg Munby, Al Leighton, Lyle Dickieson, Graham Gerry, Errin Evans, Hardy Griesbauer, Allan Lamb, John Marien, Mark Savard, Paul Berry, Roy Howard, Rick Brine, Glen Nicholson, James Taylor, Tanya Kohler, Ian King, Al Dumas, George Labrash, Craig Farnden, Mark McGirr, Marian Tamkin, Sue Bullock, Bob Van Horlick, Fergus McNab, Patty Borek, Ken Robinson, Darcy Schiller, Chad Ridsdale, Al Gamble, Dave Read, Luke Roberge, Chris Vlad, Dallas Eng, Al Huggett, Maxine Koppe, Peter Koppe, Mike Green, Heather Myers, Michael Bouris, Sean Fraser, Mike Nash, Vivien Lougheed, Kathy Plett and Greg Tyndall. A special thanks to Jordan Bacon, Melissa Read, Peter Maides and Rene Madill for their help with the editing and compilation of the book.

Thank you to the following agencies for providing us with access to their resources. Leonard DeVos and Lynne Campo of the Water Survey of Canada in Prince George and Victoria respectively, for providing us with monthly water level information on many of the rivers in this book. Birthe Miller of the Ministry of Forests for providing us with Ministry maps. Also, the College of New Caledonia for providing access to the Geography and Forestry map collections.

Also, thank you to the Cariboo Chilcotin Adventure Guides for permission to use their trip reports. As well, thanks to the Friends of Barkerville Historical Society for allowing us to reprint several of their historical articles.

How to Use This Book

This book is ordered alphabetically by trip. Additional indexes are supplied in the back of the book if the reader wants to find rivers by river rating instead of alphabetically. This may allow the reader to quickly find the trips within their skill level and possibly trips that are similar to an enjoyable trip already undertaken.

Each trip report has a standard set of sections designed to aid the reader in quickly scanning the trips, or when desired, to get additional detailed information. These sections are explained below.

Title:

The name of the trip is shown at the top of each page. This may be the name of a lake or river, or set of interconnected lakes and rivers. When a river or lake is known by more than one name, the less common name appears in brackets.

If more than one trip is described for a particular river a brief description of the overall character of the river appears before the section reports. Each trip section begins with its own title, which identifies the section.

At a Glance:

This section provides a few sentences that try to convey the general character of the trip. From this information, it is hoped that the reader may quickly determine whether or not they would like to read on to get more information.

Rating:

The river rating system used throughout this book is a North American version of the International Scale of River Difficulty used to compare river difficulty throughout the world. These guidelines offer a general classification for rivers; be aware that the system is not exact. Rivers do not always fit neatly into the various classifications, and regional interpretations of the classification system may create misunderstandings. There is no substitute for a cautious approach to rivers with which a paddler is unfamiliar. The classification system given below is taken from the Ontario Recreation Canoe Association Instructor's Manual, 2000.

Class 1: Easy
Fast moving water with riffles and small waves. Few obstructions, all are obvious and easily missed with little training. Risk to swimmers is slight; self-rescue is easy.

Class 2: Novice
Straightforward rapids with wide, clear channels which are evident without scouting.
Occasional manoeuvring may be required but rocks and medium-sized waves are easily missed by trained paddlers. Swimmers are seldom injured and group assistance, while helpful, is seldom needed. Rapids that are at the upper end of this difficulty range are designated "Class 2+"

Class 3: Intermediate
Rapids with moderate, irregular waves which may be difficult to avoid and which may swamp an open canoe. Complex manoeuvres in fast current and good boat control in tight passages or around ledges are often required; large waves or strainers may be present, but are easily avoided.

Strong eddies and powerful current effects can be found, particularly on large volume rivers. Scouting is advisable for inexperienced parties. Injuries while swimming are rare; self-rescue is usually easy, but group assistance may be required to avoid long swims. Rapids that are at the lower or upper end of this difficulty range are designated "Class III- or Class III+", respectively.

Class 4: Advanced
Intense, powerful but predictable rapids requiring precise boat handling in turbulent water. Depending on the character of the river, it may feature large, unavoidable waves and holes or constricted passages demanding fast manoeuvres under pressure. A fast, reliable eddy turn may be needed to initiate manoeuvres, scout rapids, or rest. Rapids may require "must" moves above dangerous hazards. Scouting may be necessary the first time down. Risk of injury to swimmers is moderate to high, and water conditions may make self-rescue difficult. Group assistance for rescue is often essential but requires practiced skills. A strong Eskimo roll is highly recommended. Rapids that are at the lower or upper end of this difficulty range are designated "Class IV- or Class IV+", respectively.

Class 5: Expert
Extremely long, obstructed or very violent rapids which expose a paddler to added risk. Drops may contain large, unavoidable waves and holes or steep, congested chutes with complex, demanding routes. Rapids may continue for long distances between pools, demanding a high level of fitness. What eddies exist, may be small, turbulent or difficult to reach. At the high end of the scale, several factors may be combined. Scouting is recommended, but may be difficult.

Swims are dangerous and rescue is often difficult, even for experts. A very reliable Eskimo roll, proper equipment, extensive experience, and practical rescue skills are essential. Because of the large range of difficulty that exists beyond Class IV, Class V is an open-ended, multiple level scale designated by Class 5.0, 5.1, 5.2, etc. Each of these levels is an order of magnitude more difficult than the last. Example: increasing difficulty for Class 5.0 to Class 5.1 is a similar order of magnitude as increasing from Class IV to Class V.

Class 6: Extreme and Exploratory
These runs have almost never been attempted and often exemplify the extremes of difficulty, unpredictability and danger. The consequences of error are very severe and rescue may be impossible. For teams of experts only, at favourable water levels, after close personal inspection and taking all precautions. After a Class VI rapid has been run many times, its rating may be changed to an appropriate Class 5.x rating.

Length:

The total length (distance) of the trip in kilometres from the put-in to the take-out is provided under this heading. In the case of lake trips, the length given is simply the length of the lake. This gives the reader an idea of the size of the lake, and therefore, the hazards to expect (e.g. wind). For some trips the length may be broken up into several sections based on multiple put-in/take-out options.

Time:

The time given in this section is the total time it would take to paddle the described trip from the put-in to the take-out not including breaks or play-boating time. This may be considerably different from the actual time due to varying conditions. For some trips, the time may be broken up into several sections based on multiple put-in/take-out options.

Shuttle Time:

This section indicates the time it would take to drive a shuttle vehicle one-way between the put-in and take-out. It does not include the time required to change, etc. This may help paddlers decide if alternative methods for the shuttle are possible, for instance, running or biking. Also, for some trips the shuttle time can be substantial, and is therefore, important information for trip planning.

Best Time of Year:

The best time of year for many trips is often when the water is not frozen! However, for some rivers, recommendations are made regarding water levels, and, where available, water gauge levels.

Water Flow Graphs:

For some trips the Water Survey of Canada has provided flow graphs. The bars show average m^3/second flow rate for each month. The vertical lines on the bars show the average minimum and maximum flows. These graphs can be used for planning when the best time of year is to run a river and the ranges in flow rate that you might expect.

Symbols:

There are six symbols that may appear with a trip report. The description of what each symbol indicates is provided below.

Fishing is generally good on this trip

The trip has special scenic qualities which might include canyons and rock walls or simply nice views along the way.

Plants and animals of interest are frequently seen on the trip.

The trip is mainly through a remote, wilderness region with little sign of human disturbance.

Hiking is good along either designated or non-designated hiking trails and may involve some bush-whacking to access.

The trip has features of historical significance/interest.

Hazards:

Hazards specific to this trip are listed in this section. These might include site-specific hazard locations such as a waterfall, or more general statements of hazards that might be encountered along the trip, such as log jams or sweepers. If this section is absent, for instance on lake trip reports, there are no hazards.

Maps:

Map sources for the trip are listed under this heading. The standard maps listed are the National Topographic System (NTS) 1:50,000 maps. These maps can generally be obtained through any local map dealer. In addition, the Ministry of Forest's Forest Recreation Map for the area is also listed; these maps can be very helpful in locating the access points and can be obtained from the local Ministry of Forests District or Region office. In addition to maps, some trips list other sources that may be valuable for a particular trip, such as provincial park contacts or references to local guide outfitters.

Contacts:

For trips that are circuits within a Provincial Park, such as the Bowron Lake Chain, reservations and other information are available from Super, Natural British Columbia at www.hellobc.com. Telephone: 1-800-HELLO-BC (1-800-435-5622) Toll Free Canada/USA or (250) 387-1642 for other countries.

For regular campground reservations and information check the Discover Camping Campground Reservation Service at www.discovercamping.ca. Telephone: 1-800-689-9025. The BC Parks web site can also be very helpful, www.elp.gov.bc.ca/bcparks.

Note that not all campgrounds currently accept reservations. For information on these parks contact BC Parks Prince George Office, Box 2045 (4051 18th Ave.), Prince George, BC, V2N 2J6. Telephone: (250) 565-6340. A park map is usually also available at the parks' information booths.

To obtain Ministry of Forests Recreation Maps check the Provincial Ministry of Forests website at www.gov.bc.ca/for. Follow the links to find the Region or District Office of interest. Otherwise, to obtain Ministry of Forests Region or District Office contacts telephone Enquiry BC Toll Free in BC at 1-800-663-7867. Elsewhere call (604) 660-2421.

Getting There:

This section provides the directions to the trip along the main roads. Directions are always given starting from Prince George, home of Mr. P.G!

Put-in:

This section details how to get to the put-in for the trip. This is often along small, difficult to find roads. For some shorter trips, an alternate put-in may be described. Access to the put-in locations is usually described by the order they are encountered when driving the road.

Access:

For longer trips with many options for put-in and take-out locations, access points will be numbered based on when they are encountered when traveling down the river.

Take-out:

This section details how to get to the take-out for the trip. This is often along small, difficult to find roads. For some trips, an alternate take-out may be described. The take-out description may appear before the put-in description if it is reached first when accessing the river; this may help in planning the shuttle.

Description:

This section provides a description of what to expect on any given trip. Hazards, along with any other special features, are highlighted. Rapid locations and ratings, as well as portage options, are described. However, in most cases, how to run the rapid is not described. It is up to the reader to evaluate his or her own paddling skills as well as the groups' and then decide how to run, or not run, a rapid.

Camping:

Options for camping near the trip access points are provided, including a brief description and directions. For overnight or longer trips, some general recommendations for camping during the trip are made but without great detail.

Arctic - Pacific Lake Chain

At a Glance: This lake chain comprises Arctic, Portage and Pacific Lakes situated in the Misinchinka Ranges on the continental divide. Portage and Pacific Lakes are accessible only by portaging and have plenty of fish.

Best time: late May to October. Some years ice may still be on the lake towards the end of May.

Maps: 93-I/5, Prince George Forest District Map

Getting There: From Prince George, drive north on Highway 97. Approximately 22km after Summit Lake (just before the level railway crossing on Highway 97) turn right off Highway 97 into The Pas Lumber Hart Sawmill. Pass through the mill site (staying just to the right of the weigh scales) to the start of the 700 Chuchinka Road. Use caution and obey all signs when traveling through the mill area. At 55km, turn right onto Chuchinka-Arctic Forest Service Road. Continue on this road for 28km to the put-in as described below.

Put-in: You will cross the Parsnip River at 73km of the Chuchinka-Arctic Forest Service Road. At 79km of the Chuchinka-Arctic Forest Service Road, stay right on the 700 Road. At 81.5km you again come to a bridge over the Parsnip River; put-in here. All roads are two-wheel drive though clearance may be required. Paddle down the Parsnip River for approximately 4km to where a creek flows into (or sometimes out of) the Parsnip River on river left. It is the only creek you will encounter along this stretch of the Parsnip River. Paddling is easy up this gently flowing creek that meanders through a marsh area. Stay right at the only junction in the creek and paddle for 3km to Arctic Lake.

Take-out: At the put-in, which requires paddling approximately 4km up the Parsnip River.

Rating: Class 1

Length:
5km Arctic Lake
10km Pacific Lake

Time: 2 to 3 days

Hazards:
•power boats
•sweepers

Alternate Take-out: The Parsnip River Bridge at 73km of the Chuchinka-Arctic Forest Service Road. This is approximately 21km downstream from the creek that joins the Parsnip River to Arctic Lake and takes approximately 3 to 4 hours to paddle to from the Lake.

Description: This lake chain is comprised of the Arctic, Portage, and Pacific Lakes. The lakes are situated on the Arctic-Pacific continental divide and are part of the Alexander Mackenzie route. Arctic Lake is often ice-free on or about the end of May. The other lakes follow within a few weeks. The lakes are very narrow and the beautiful Misinchinka Ranges of the Rocky Mountains rise from their shorelines offering tempting alpine ridge hikes. Access to the alpine is best from Pacific Lake. Arctic Lake is the longest of the three at approximately 5km. Portage and Pacific Lakes are 2.5km long. Riverboats can access Arctic Lake while a short, rough portage (less than 500m) found at the end of Arctic Lake on the left (north-east) side keeps Portage and Pacific Lakes remote. To access Pacific Lake from Portage Lake you can drag your loaded canoe over a few logs and beaver dams and float down a 100m long small creek.

Wayne Giles

The May long weekend isn't always late enough for paddling Arctic Lake

Marian Tamkin

Portage Lake is part of the Alexander Mackenzie Heritage Canoe Route.

Camping: Undeveloped campsites exist throughout the lakes. The nicest site is at a rocky point on the north-east shore of Arctic Lake approximately 400m from the mouth of the creek when paddling into the lakes. There is also a site directly across from this site on the other shore. Other campsites are located on Arctic Lake about half way down the lake on the north-east and south-west shores. Camping is available at both ends of the portage trail connecting Arctic and Portage Lakes though neither are recommended. No campsites exist on Portage Lake. Pacific Lake has two campsites located on the north-east shore of the lake on points extending into the lakes. One is very sheltered in the trees and the other on an exposed but beautiful point. In addition to campsites on the Arctic Lakes circuit, camping is also available at many Forest Service Sites in the region.

Rivers of the Central Interior

A group of eight skilled paddlers in a single voyageur canoe, decided to challenge the Rivers of the Central Interior. They crossed the border into B.C. on May 18 and paddled up the Peace River. The river was swift and paddling upstream was brutal. The river got rough and they had to do an ugly portage near Hudson's Hope. Finally, on May 31, they reached the confluence of the Finlay and Parsnip Rivers. Turning south, they paddled up to the headwaters of the Parsnip and reached Arctic Lake on June 12. They then portaged over the continental divide and put into James Creek.

Unfortunately, they had not obtained adequate information in advance and the next day, they found themselves in trouble. Unable to handle the violent rapids, they capsized, wrecking their canoe and losing some of their supplies. Luckily, no one was hurt, but they were scared and wanted to abandon the trip. However, the trip leader talked them into patching the canoe and they continued downstream.

They were much more cautious this time, portaging frequently and moving downstream slowly. After two days, the river became much smoother and they paddled down Herrick Creek, the McGregor River, and finally, the Fraser River, which took them to Prince George. On June 19, when they reached the mouth of the Nechako River they were in early morning fog and couldn't even see the Nechako.

They paddled downstream until June 22, when they met some locals who told them that they were crazy if they thought they could paddle the ugly rapids at Hell's Gate, and politely suggested instead that the paddlers would be better off staying on dry land. Wisely, they decided not to proceed downstream, and they paddled back up to the mouth of the Blackwater River. On July 4, tired of paddling, they stashed their canoe and went for a hike along the Blackwater River, scrambled over some mountains, and eventually reached the west coast. There, they found an old rock and wrote on it, "Alexander Mackenzie, from Canada by land, 22nd July, 1793".

Baker Creek

At a Glance: This is a low volume creek. The upper section contains a 2 metre waterfall and 2 significant rapids. It is a short, technical run that often contains several river wide logs. Below the main rapids there is 40km of scenic Class 2 to 3 water that winds past Pinnacles Provincial Park and ends at the Fraser River in West Quesnel.

Best Time of Year: Baker Creek is fed primarily by rain and local snowmelt. The local runoff creates high water early in the spring, usually lasting until the end of May. Continuous heavy rains will bring the water level back up later in the season. The best time for a first run is in the medium flows that usually occur in June. In August the creek is often too low to float down.

Rating:
•low water - Class 3+ to 4
•medium water - Class 4+
•high water - Class 5

Length: 1.5km

Time: 0.5 to 1.5 hours

Shuttle time: 20 minutes

Hazards:
•logjams
•sweepers
•rocks
•fast water

Maps: 93-B/15, Cariboo Forest Region Recreation Map

Getting There: From Prince George, drive 120km south on Highway 97 to Quesnel. (Even though there is no gauge, you can check water levels next to the Toyota dealership in West Quesnel, 1km past the bridge over the Fraser River). Once in Quesnel, cross the Fraser River on the Moffat Bridge and turn right at the first exit. Continue straight up the road (North Fraser Road which becomes the Nazko Highway) for 30.3 kilometres to a large gravel pit. 300m off the highway at the edge of the gravel pit a 200m trail to the creek starts.

Put-in/Take-out: The put in and take out are within 400 metres of each other at opposite ends of the gravel pit. The main rapids circle around the pit creating a very short shuttle. Go through the gate at the gravel pit and keep right for 300m. Park at the far right corner of the gravel pit. A 200m trail leads down the hill along the fence line. The put-in is 100 metres upstream from the end of the fence (20m above the waterfall).

Alternate Put-in: It is possible to put-in 15km upstream. Turn left onto Tibbles Road 200 metres past Sylvia's Café (10km from the gravel pit) and drive 4km to the bridge over Baker Creek. The upper section offers scenic Class 2 to 2+ water with occasional river-wide log jams.

Alternate Take-out: If you want to run the lower 40km of the creek, an alternate take-out exists behind West Park Mall, 1.0km past the end of the Fraser River Bridge in West Quesnel. Watch for creek wide log jams throughout this section.

Description: The river starts with a steep 2-metre high waterslide with a fairly grabby horizontal hole at the bottom. Run this with lots of speed and avoid the logs and rocks on river left.

Dallas Eng

Graham Gerry makes the first descent of Log Jam at low flows

Below the waterfall, Class 2 rapids lead around a sharp right corner. Eddy out on river right 50 metres past the corner. The next rapid, Logjam (Class 4), requires manoeuvring around rocks, small ledge drops, and the logs that give the rapid its name.

A few hundred metres below Logjam the creek turns left again and starts to drop through the most technical section of the river, The Staircase. Eddy out and scout on river left when you see the orange flagging tape that signals the start of the Staircase. This rapid consists of a fairly steep boulder garden that requires continuous manoeuvring for 100m. The consequences of flipping over in this section could be substantial. In high water this stretch of water is Class 5. In July 2000, several river wide logs were located in the Class 3 exit rapids of the Staircase.

Take out on river left after you have run the main rapids (any Class 2 and 3 you paddle below the Staircase can add a lot of time to the walk out), and carry your boat for 20 minutes up-hill to the gravel pit.

Camping: There is a provincial campground at Puntchesakut Lake 8 kilometres up the highway from the gravel pit. There is also a good campground with a sandy beach at Ten Mile Lake Provincial Park 10km north of Quesnel on Highway 97.

Beaumont Provincial Park

At a Glance: Located on the east end of Fraser Lake where the Nautley River exits the lake. Lake paddling, fishing and playing in the Nautley River are all possible.

Maps: 93-K/2, Vanderhoof Forest District Recreation Map

Getting There: From Prince George, drive west approximately 135km on Highway 97 to the town of Fort Fraser. Three kilometres west of Fort Fraser turn right to Beaumont Provincial Park.

Description: Play in the beach area or choose to explore some of the lake shoreline. The Nautley River (see Nautley River/Nechako River trip report) flows out of Fraser Lake near the park and is a nice area to explore. Be careful not to venture too far down the river as the current picks up quickly before the bridge.

Camping: Full facility camping is available though no sites have lake frontage.

Hazards:
- power boats
- high winds

Best time:
May to October

Rick Brine

One-way only please! The Nechako River flooding Cottonwood Island Park.

Blackwater River

Famous for its fishing, this river is also a whitewater canoe tripper's delight! A well-kept B.C. secret, this river provides some of the finest extended wilderness tripping and whitewater canoeing in the province. A fantastic mix of scenic lake travel, exciting river paddling, great fishing and adventure, this river has it all!

The river is broken down into four separate trip descriptions. For those looking for an exciting extended wilderness canoe trip, the upper section from Eliguk Lake to Nazko Bridge is unrivalled in British Columbia. The last three trip descriptions can be run as single day whitewater canoe trips. The section from Nazko Bridge to Batnuni Bridge offers intermediate/beginner whitewater paddling while the last two sections down to the Fraser River offer advanced/intermediate whitewater.

Marian Tamkin

One of the many waterfalls on the river, Kusyuko Falls has a spectacular campsite located at its brink.

Eliguk Lake to Nazko Bridge

At a Glance: The wilderness canoeing on this stretch of the river is superb! A very nice mix of lake and river travel, interspersed with whitewater and portaging, make this section very entertaining and a true adventure. Fishing opportunities abound.

Best Time of Year: medium water level. Lower water levels can involve extensive lining. Levels vary greatly with the amount of rain.

Maps: 93-C/14, 93-C/15, 93-F/2, 93-F/1, 93-G/4, 93-G/3, Cariboo Forest Region Recreation Map (West)

Getting there: There are numerous options for starting points with Eliguk Lake being the furthest upstream and the location with which this trip description begins. All options involve arranging air service from numerous locations including Nimpo Lake, Williams Lake and Burns Lake. Nimpo Lake is the closest by air to the river and the most common trip staging area.

Put-in: Fly into Eliguk Lake and land at the campsite at the west end of the lake.

Rating: Class 3 to 3+

Length: 165km

Time:10days

Hazards:
- waterfalls
- difficult rapids
- difficult portages
- prone to floods

Alternate Put-in: Tsacha Lake is an alternate location for starting the trip and reduces the trip by 48km, and approximately 2 days travel time. Land at the sandy point on the south shore across from an island near the west end of the lake. There are many other lakes to land at downstream of this location if you wish to shorten the trip further.

Take-out: The first location with road access to take-out at is the Nazko Bridge across the Blackwater River, 85km upstream of the Fraser River (see map sheet 93-G/4).

Description: Given the nature of this trip, it is important that paddlers research the route prior to departure. This description can only provide a summary, as the river deserves a book of its own.

The description has been broken into sections based on major lakes along the route. Beside the heading of each section, an estimate of the time it took a group to paddle the section in medium water is given as a reference. This is time on the water as well as portages. It does not include breaks/lunch.

Eliguk Lake to Tsasha Lake (19 hours)

Eliguk Lake offers views of Tundra Mountain in the Ilgachuz Range, the headwaters of the Blackwater River, and more distant views of the Rainbow Range in Tweedsmuir Provincial Park. Fishing is good and access can be gained to the Alexander Mackenzie Heritage Trail (AMT) on the north shore of the lake. For a short day hike, follow the trail west to Basalt Lake and the basalt towers there. Paddle to the east end of the lake and take out in a clearing on the north shore at the start of beaver-dam-filled Ulgako Creek. An easy 2km portage follows a wagon road. Look for the start of

Wayne Giles

Pack light! There are many portages if paddling the headwaters of the river.

the road north over the hill in the clearing and follow the road to a cabin near Geese Lake. Look for a small drainage just past the cabin; this leads through the swamp to Geese Lake and provides an easy route for canoes. Just downstream of Geese Lake, the

Blackwater River flows from the south and joins Ulgako Creek. The river is basically a creek at this point, narrow and meandering for the next 5km to an abandoned bridge across the river that must be portaged. A second cabin is passed 8km downstream from the bridge where Carnlick Creek flows into the river from the south. This creek doubles the size of the river though it still flows gently.

Downstream of Carnlick Creek another bridge crosses the river. Mark this location, as a rapid is located 2.5km downstream. This rapid can be portaged/lined on river left. After this rapid, the river meanders through some remote farmland with homesteads until another bridge (metal, very good condition) crosses the river. Pull out above the bridge and scout the rapids downstream from the wagon road on river right. This rapid is a short boulder garden.

Be aware that 2.5km below the above rapid there is a rapid with a mandatory portage around a waterfall. The rapid leading up to the waterfall is located at the very top of the river on map 93C15, approximately 7km upstream of Tsasha Lake. Take out at the start

Barbara Robertson

Lining your canoe and bushwacking are all part of the fun on the upper stretches of the river.

of this rapid and scout on river left. Make sure you scout all the way to the waterfall as it comes up quickly! The rapid is a series of shallow ledges with several islands. Portage the waterfall on river left. Immediately below the falls the river is narrow with log jams; portaging is recommended.

Downstream of the waterfall, the river calms and meanders into 21km long Tsasha Lake. A superb campsite is located at the sandy point along the south shore 3km from the west end of the lake. You might even try either the Blackwater Lodge or Mackenzie Trail Lodge for cold beverages! Another campsite is available at a small cabin (maintained by the Mackenzie Trail Lodge) at the east end of the lake. Paddlers are welcome.

Tsasha Lake to Euchiniko Lakes (15 hours)
Leaving Tsasha Lake is the most popular section of the river for fishing. A well-used trail follows the shore on river right. Use this trail to scout the rapid immediately downstream. Scout downstream to around a bend to the right where a steep-walled canyon starts that contains significant ledges and holes. The first section of the rapid can be portaged/lined on the right. Portage the canyon on river left (some bushwhacking) or river right (over high canyon walls and loose boulder terrain).

Put in below the canyon and paddle 1km to where the rapids start leading up to the spectacular Kusyuko Falls, a mandatory portage (located 2.5km upstream of Euchiniko Lakes). Pull out at the start of the rapid on river right well above the falls and scout down to the falls. An incredible campsite is located along the portage trail at the brink of the falls with great fishing below. The rapid leaving the pool below the falls contains some large haystacks and should be scouted from river right.

Euchiniko Lakes are a series of three narrow lakes joined by short swifts. The lakes total nearly 30km in length. Camping on the lakes is somewhat scarce and restricted to sites with cabins, some maintained while others abandoned. The most promising site is located at the cabins 2km past Kluskus Creek.

Euchiniko Lakes to Nazko Bridge (11 hours)
The river section between Euchiniko Lakes and Kluskoil Lake moves along quickly with long sections of entertaining Class 2 to 2+ rapids. Camping is available high on a bank at a bend in the river 6km upstream of Kluskoil Lake. Paddle 8km through the interesting esker formations of Kluskoil Lake to the landing at Kluskoil Lake Provincial Park near Chinee Falls (camping is available). There is a small group of cabins above and below the falls. Scout the rapids/falls from river left. Make sure you scout the entire rapids as it ends in a second set of falls 0.5km downstream of the first set of falls. The first set of falls can be portaged on river left. If you choose to run the section between the falls, the second set of falls can be portaged easily on river right. After Chinee Falls, the next 35km downstream to the Nazko Bridge across the Blackwater River is Class 1 to 2+.

Camping: If landing at Eliguk Lake, both the very west end and east end of the lake offer good camping. Along the river, camping is found at good intervals at unorganized sites and lodges/cabins.

One of the biggest challenges on the river is dodging the many hard to see black rocks.

Nazko Bridge to Batnuni Bridge (or Gillies Crossing)

At a Glance: This section of the river is an enjoyable paddle through forested shorelines interspersed with a few hayfields. Take your time and try a little fishing.

Best time: after spring run-off.

Maps: 93-G/4, 93-G/5, Cariboo Forest Region Recreation Map (West)

Getting there: From Prince George, drive a short distance west on Highway 16 to the Blackwater Road turnoff on the left. Drive for 34km passing through the town of Baldy Hughes to a fork in the road. Take the right fork marked Blackwater Road. Drive a further 13.5km to a second fork and take the right fork. 19km from the second fork, you will reach the Blackwater Bridge crossing the Blackwater River (a total of 71km from Highway 16).

Take-out: Continue over the Blackwater River Bridge driving for 4km and turn right onto Batnuni Road. Drive 25km on this road to the Batnuni Bridge across the Blackwater River; this is the take-out.

Rating: Class 1 to 1+ optional 2+ to 3+ rapid

Length: 26km

Time: 6 hours

Hazards: hidden rocks

Shuttle time: 20 minutes

Alternate take-out: Cross the Batnuni Bridge over the Blackwater River and drive another 5.4km to Nazko road; turn left and drive 1.2km to the take-out at Gillies Crossing. This bridge crosses the Euchiniko River, which at this point is more a lake to its confluence with the Blackwater River 2km southeast.

Put-in: Continue on the Nazko Road another 17.5km to the Nazko Bridge across the Blackwater River.

Description: The Blackwater River is a small river after spring runoff is finished, alternating from easy riffles to shallow pools in this portion with less than 100ft. elevation drop over 24km. The Nazko River enters on the right soon after the start of the run. The shoreline is mostly forested with a few hay fields; cattle are sometimes seen as well as wildlife. At 22km, the river turns sharply left and a wide, grassy slough appears on river left, which is the mouth of the Euchiniko River. At this point you have two options: paddling to Gillies Crossing on the Euchiniko River or continuing on the Blackwater River to the Batnuni Bridge.

To finish your trip at Gillies Crossing, turn up the Euchiniko River, which narrows into a very slow channel then opens out into the lake that is visible from Gillies Crossing. If instead you decide to continue downstream to the Batnuni Bridge, be prepared for the rapids starting 1.5km upstream of the Batnuni Bridge. There is a short canyon with Class 2+ to 3+ rapids that should be scouted. A trail to the road leaves the river on river left just above the rapids and can be used for portaging. However, it is not recommended as it is a steep climb to the road and a long portage back to the river at the bridge.

Camping: At the put-in or take-out. Numerous forest recreation sites are also in the area. Unorganized camping is available along the river.

John Marien

The 4-foot wide slot. Be sure to pull in your paddle!

Batnuni Bridge to Blackwater Bridge

At a Glance: Lots of play time with boulder gardens and rapids galore. This is a technical portion of the river and best paddled with someone who has run it before.

Best Time of Year: medium to low water. Though the paddling season varies greatly with the amount of rain, usually June or later.

Maps: 93-G/6, Cariboo Forest Region Recreation Map (West)

Getting there: From Prince George, drive a short distance west on Highway 16 to the Blackwater Road turnoff on the left, which is marked with a sign to West Lake Provincial Park. Drive 34km through the town of Baldy Hughes to a fork in the road. Take the right fork marked Blackwater Road. Drive a further 13.5km to a second fork and take the right fork. 19km from the second fork you will reach the Blackwater Bridge crossing the Blackwater River (a total of 71km from Highway 16).

Take-out: At the Blackwater Bridge across the river as described above.

Put-in: Continue over the Blackwater River Bridge driving for 4km and turn right onto Batnuni Road. Drive 25km on this road to the Batnuni Bridge across the Blackwater River; this is the put-in.

Description: The Blackwater River in this section is a low volume, but very technical, river that demands respect by paddlers in open boats. It is recommended that a paddler who knows the river accompany a first run. If this is not possible, all major rapids and drops should be scouted before running. This river is not recommended for paddlers in closed boats due to the large amount of Class 1 paddling.

Rating: Class 2 to 3

Length: 31km

Time: 7 to 8 hours

Shuttle time: 30 minutes

Hazards:
- sharp rocks difficult to see
- log jams
- changing water levels

The first 6.5km are Class 1 with one easy Class 2 section, a good place to warm up for the sections to follow. Next, the river follows a large horseshoe bend, Class 2, and splits around an island. The river then approaches gravel cut-banks and bends sharply to the right. There is a large, quiet pool on river left before the bend and on the bend there is a Class 2 rapid that should be scouted for log jams.

The river splits around another island and flows in an 'S' pattern. Avoid the headwalls on each outside bend. A split around another island follows this. When the river approaches the gravel cut-banks a second time, stay on river right and eddy-out well above the right bend in the river. Scout around the bend. The rapid below is Class 3 and is the start of a section of the river containing 4 major pool drops. Be prepared to pull out and scout at anytime in this section. The first drop (Class 2+ to 3) is preceded by a boulder garden as the river bends to the left. The second drop (Class 2+ to 3) has a large boulder midstream with a strong boiling eddy behind it. The third drop (Class 3) contains ledges on river left and river right and boulders throughout. At low water, it is possible to run it on the extreme right over a 1 metre (3') drop. Lining is possible but difficult. The fourth drop (Class 3) has a definite 'V' midstream but it piles into a boulder.

There is a Class 2 rapid below this section starting just above an island. The island signifies the end of the pool-drop section. The river then calms to Class 1+ for 2km then picks up velocity for approximately 2km of Class 2 to 2+ rapids. There is a good campsite on river left at the bottom of the first rapid in this section. The river mellows again with Class 1+ to 2 rapids over the next 7km.

Watch for the approach to the second canyon; the river bends to the left where there is a large hole on river left and then it straightens. Eddy-out on river left, well above the right bend in the river and scout. The canyon starts with the Hallway, a significant drop followed by large standing waves. The river narrows at one point to 4 feet though the water is relatively calm through the slot (see previous picture). After the slot, there is a short boulder garden and the rapids end.

Below the canyon to the bridge at the take-out, the river is Class 1+ with some easy Class 2 sections. Eddy-out on river left immediately below the bridge.

Note on high water:
It is possible to run this section when water levels are high but only by a strong group of advanced paddlers that are familiar with the river. Some of the rapids described above become easier as boulders and other obstacles are buried, and some rapids become more difficult as the velocity of the river increases into headwalls.

The rapid immediately preceding the pool-drop section becomes more difficult as the water piles into a log jam on river left. It is difficult to hug river right around the bend, and a swim here would be nasty due to the log jam and rapids downstream.

The river bends sharply with regularity in this section; headwalls are ever present and should be treated cautiously. The second canyon must be scouted from river left to ensure there are no logs jamming the 4' wide slot. The approach to the canyon is very pushy and the holes are ugly. Large standing waves are waiting to swamp an open boat. Once inside the canyon, the hydraulics become turbulent, particularly in the eddy on river right above the 4' slot. The 4' slot becomes a clean 1 metre drop into a pool below.

Camping: Forest Service Recreation Site at the take-out.
Unorganized at put-in and along river.

Blackwater River – Blackwater Bridge to Fraser River

At a Glance: This paddle is virtually unparalleled in B.C. for open boat, whitewater, and river running. This section takes you through spectacular canyons with plentiful rapids and play spots. Bring your fishing rod as the fishing is great! It is a river you will want to keep coming back to.

Best Time of Year: medium to low water. Though the paddling season varies greatly with the amount of rain, usually June or later.

Maps: 93-G/6, 93-G/7, Cariboo Forest Region Recreation Map (West)

Getting there: From Prince George, drive a short distance west on Highway 16 to the Blackwater Road turnoff on the left. Drive 34km through the town of Baldy Hughes to a fork in the road. Take the right fork marked Blackwater Road. Drive a further 13.5km to a second fork, "marker 20."

Take-out: At "marker 20," turn left to get to the take-out and for the shuttle drop off. At 21km there is a fork in the road; stay left for another 4.3km till you come to an old logging landing on the Fraser River. Drive vehicles as far downstream of this landing as possible.

Drive back along the road from the landing to a fork in the road near the top of the hill. Take the left fork and continue driving along this road for 21.2kms where it rejoins the Blackwater Road. From here, turn left and it is 3.2kms to the Blackwater Bridge.

Because it is difficult to paddle up the Fraser River and reach this take-out, it is recommended that an alternate site be investigated downstream on the Fraser River.

Rating: Class: 3

Length: 28km

Time 8 to 10 hours

Shuttle time: 45 minutes

Hazards:
- remote canyon
- log jams
- high water on Fraser
- sharp rocks difficult to see
- changing water levels

Put-in: At the Blackwater Bridge.

Description: This section of the river is very tricky at the start with tight Class 2+ hairpin bends before entering a Class 1 canyon. Past the canyon, the river splits around an island. Take the left channel (the right channel is impassable) and proceed with caution, eddying out on river left immediately above the approaching Class 3 rapid. Scout this rapid from river left. The rapid contains mid-stream boulders, a significant hole, and cliffs/headwalls. Much of the rapid can be lined on river left if necessary.

Following this rapid, the next 2km of the river is Class 1+ to 2 before the start of the second canyon. This canyon is 14km long and contains numerous Class 2 to 2+ rapids. Pool drops, headwalls, large standing waves, holes, and ledges are all encountered, and scouting is recommended throughout.

Just past the halfway point of the trip (17km downstream of the put-in bridge) there is evidence of a large slide on river right, and below this there is the first decent camping spot located on river right. After the slide, the rapids in the next 3km are Class 2+ boulder gardens. The river then mellows for 4km before the last canyon.

Ken Robinson

A typical stretch of the river, canyon walls, swift rapids and plenty of eddies.

Tako Creek marks the entrance to the last canyon. The velocity increases and the river narrows around a sharp right hairpin bend. Keep to river left and eddy-out immediately above the start of the Class 2+ to 3 canyon. Again, this canyon has numerous features to avoid, including holes and large standing waves.

Below the final canyon, the river becomes Class 1 until reaching the Fraser River. The take-out is on river right of the Fraser River, 2km upstream of the confluence of the Blackwater and Fraser Rivers. There are two options from the confluence. The first is to ferry across the Fraser River, paddle up river left until you are well upstream of your shuttle vehicle, and ferry back to the take-out. The second option is to paddle upstream on river right. This option is only possible in tandem boats with enough power to paddle upstream against the Fraser River current. There are two or three spots where the current is too strong for solo paddlers.

Camping:
Camping is available at a Forest Service Site at the put-in. Unorganized camping is available along the river. Sites are almost non-existent for first 18km but plentiful after that.

Ken Robinson

Camping and fishing are excellent at the outflow of Tsacha Lake.

Bowron Lake Chain

At a Glance: Bowron Lake Provincial Park is a magnificent wilderness area nestled in the Cariboo Mountains southeast of Prince George. It offers a unique circular chain of lakes, creeks, and rivers (and 8 portages). Its popularity attracts visitors from around the world, which can make it crowded at times, but it also invites camaraderie.

Best time of year: Paddling is possible from May to October, but the most popular time is July and August. Canoeists must register and pay from mid May to mid September. A quota system permits only 55 people or 27 canoes to start each day, so be prepared to wait a day or two if you haven't registered in advance.

Maps: 93-H/2, 93-H/3, 93-H/6, 93-H/7, Quesnel Forest District Recreation Map. Park Headquarters provides a map showing the location of campsites. Other information, as well as reservations are available from Super Natural British Columbia at www.hellobc.com Telephone: 1-800-HELLO-BC. Books have been published on this lake chain, so consult these for more detailed descriptions.

Getting there: From Prince George, drive south on Highway 97 for 88km, then turn left onto the Barkerville Highway (Highway 26). A short distance past Wells, turn left and follow signs to Bowron Lakes Provincial Park, 28km further, on a good gravel road.

Rating: Class 1 to 2

Length:
total - 116km
six portages from 0.4 to 2.8km

Time 6 to 10 days

Hazards:
•wind
•snow in spring and fall
•dead heads on Cariboo R
•sweepers on Cariboo R

Description: Most of the portaging on this chain is done within the first few days. Fortunately, this is relatively easy because trails are well maintained and allow the use of canoe carts. The trip starts with a 2.4km portage to Kibbee Lake, a short paddle down Kibbee Lake, and another 2km portage to Indianpoint Lake. Indianpoint Lake is separated from Isaac Lake by a 1.6km portage. These three lakes are clear and a beautiful aquamarine color. A moderate day's travel will get you to Indianpoint Lake and a strenuous day's travel will get you to Wolverine Bay on Isaac Lake. Isaac Lake is long and narrow and surrounded by beautiful mountains. There are numerous campsites along the east shore. Allow two days to paddle this lake.

Isaac River flows out of Isaac Lake and is Class 2. It starts with the Chute where the river drops between two rocky ledges and then makes a sharp right turn. Below the Chute, the Class is 1+ to the first portage at the Cascades. The river drops many vertical metres over the impassable Cascades and then mellows again to Class 1+ to the waterfall. The waterfall must also be portaged. This portage trail is steep but provides an excellent view of the falls on a small side trail.

Isaac River to McLeary Lake takes a half to a full day, depending on how many portage carries you make. If you do single carries, a solid day of canoeing and portaging may take you to Lanezi Lake. McLeary

Wayne Giles

The Park is known for its magnificent mountain views

Chris Vlad

Sailing can be the best way to get down the long and often windy lakes

Lake is the most beautiful of the eleven lakes, offering crystal clear water and a panorama of rugged mountains. At the south end of the lake, the Cariboo River enters. This Class 2 river is swift and cold and full of glacier silt, so it is impossible to see submerged rocks and deadheads. Remain alert while paddling this section.

Lanezi Lake is silty but still offers mountain scenery. Campsites are fewer, so it is not advisable to travel if the wind is threatening. Watch for shallows and deadheads in the narrows between Lanezi and Sandy Lakes. At Sandy Lake, the scenery changes to rolling hills. The lake is fairly shallow and prone to huge waves on windy days. A very slow-moving portion of the Cariboo River without unusual hazards joins Sandy and Una Lakes. Watch for a narrow entrance on river left to Una Lake. It is well worth the short hike from Una Lake to the 24 metre Cariboo Falls.

From Una Lake, you will have to backtrack 400m upstream on the Cariboo River to the mouth of Babcock Creek. This creek must be portaged in order to protect fish. Spectacle Lake is bordered by rolling hills and has shallows, marshes, sandy beaches and warm water. At the end of this lake, the Bowron River flows gently through marshes for 4km to Bowron Lake. Expect to see beaver and a variety of birds in the marshes. The north end of Bowron Lake marks the end of the trip; take out at the boat launch.

Shorter trips are possible by starting at the north end of Bowron Lake and paddling toward Spectacle Lake (referred to as the west side). If you enjoy watching birds and mammals such as beaver and moose, there is a campsite in the marshy section that connects Bowron and Spectacle Lakes. You can be almost certain to spot a variety of wildlife, especially during an evening paddle. This trip is appropriate for a two day weekend. If you have three days, you can travel to Pat's Point on Spectacle Lake and enjoy the large beach and, in summer, the warm water.

Camping: There are 54 marked campsites throughout the circuit, 4 with cooking shelters and 9 with non-cooking shelters in various states of repair. Groups with 4 to 7 canoes must use sites designated for group use. A 7 day camping itinerary is provided to groups before they embark. If you must wait a day or two before starting, there is a provincial campground at the start of the circuit and two provincial campgrounds near Barkerville. Three private lodges and canoe outfitters are also located at the north end of Bowron Lake.

Bowron River

At a Glance: With its clear water, deep pools, canyons and rapids, the Bowron is a beautiful and challenging river to paddle. It begins in the Cariboo Mountains of Bowron Lakes Provincial Park then flows north to the Fraser River, skirting the western edge of the Cariboo Range. Before the 1980s, canoeists recognized the high recreational value of this river and suggested it should be preserved as a wild river. Unfortunately, extensive logging has occurred since then and logging roads run along most of the river. Many vistas show large clear cuts that now contain young forests. The area supports a variety of wildlife, including a healthy run of spring salmon in late summer.

A number of shorter trips are possible on the Bowron. A very popular white water day trip begins at Portage Canyon and runs to Lyle's Lawn (described in a separate report). The section from Tsus Creek to Highway 16 is a good day trip for canoeists who are comfortable paddling the Class 2+ rapids just upstream of the take-out. These rapids can be avoided by taking out at an old coal mine site. The section from Haggen Creek to Highway 16 is a great weekend trip, and would be suitable for people with basic paddling skills if they took out at the old coal mine site. It would also be possible for intermediate paddlers to start at the bridge 14 km upstream from the Haggen Creek junction in order to paddle through the impressive canyon.

Rating: Class 1 to 3+

Length:182km

Time: 1 week

Shuttle time: 4 hours

Hazards:
- log jam and sweepers
- canyons difficult to line or portage
- dramatic water changes after heavy rains

Length and time for sections

Bowron Lake to Fraser River:	181km	6 to7 days
Bowron Lake to Haggen Creek:	54km	2 days
Haggen Creek to Highway 16:	60km	2 days
Haggen Creek to Tsus Creek:	33km	5 hours
Tsus Creek to Coal Mine:	10km	2.5 hours
Coal Mine to Highway 16:	17km	3 hours
Highway 16 to Box Canyon:	24km	6 to 7 hours
Box Canyon to Fraser River:	43km	2 days

Water Flow Rates

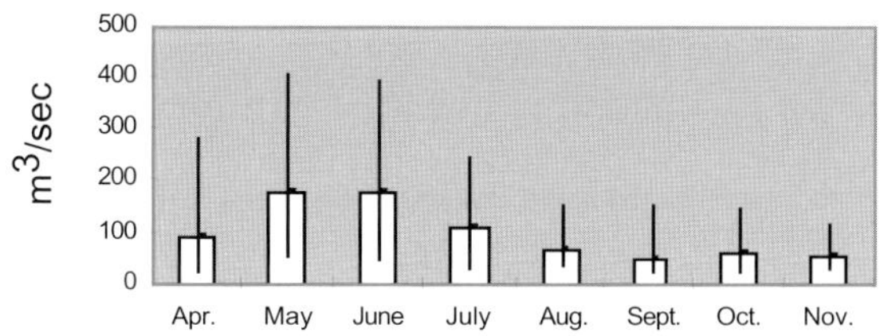

Best time of year: July to October, some canyons are difficult to run or to line in higher water. Flow rates taken below Box Canyon.

Maps: 93-H/6, 93-H/5, 93-H/12, 93-H/13, BC Ministry of Forests: Prince George Forest District recreation map

Getting there: To access the first put-in, at Bowron Lake, take Highway 97 south from Prince George and just before arriving in Quesnel turn left onto Highway 26. A few kilometres after Wells, turn left and follow signs to Bowron Lake Provincial Park. All other put-ins can be accessed from Highway 16 east of Prince George.

Put-in - Bowron Lake: The road to park headquarters crosses Bowron River just past Bowron Lake Lodge at the north end of Bowron Lake. Purists may want to paddle a further 7km across Bowron Lake, 4km through Bowron Slough, and up the Bowron River as far as navigation is permitted (the upper reaches have been closed to canoeists to protect wildlife.)

Access #1: Access to this put-in is from Highway 16. Drive east from Prince George for 55km to the bridge that crosses the Bowron River (access #5). Just after crossing the bridge turn right, and then left at the T-junction onto the Beaver Forest Road. Continue on this road, turning right at the junction with Bowron Forest Service road. Drive over the bridge that crosses the Bowron close to Haggen Creek and put in at the next bridge, which is approximately 15km further (stay left at the junction with Narrow Forest Service Road).

Access #2 - Haggen Creek Forest Service Recreation Site: From the T-junction described for access #1, turn left onto the Beaver Forest Road. Turn right at the Bowron Forest Service Road. The put-in at Haggen Creek Forest Service Recreation Site is 50km from Highway 16.

Access #3 - Tsus Creek: From the T-junction described for access #1, turn left onto the Beaver Forest Road; drive approximately 16km and turn right onto a poorly marked road that leads quickly to the river. It is also possible to access this point from river left, a good option if you plan to take out at the old coal mine site. From Highway 16, turn right onto the Cut-Off Forest Road (2km before the Bowron River bridge). Follow the Cut-Off road 7.4km to a fork. Take the left fork; drive 13km then turn onto a side road on the left. The river is 1.3km down this road.

Access #4 - Old Coal Mine Site: From Highway 16, turn right onto the Cut-Off Forest Road 2km before the Bowron River bridge. Follow the Cut-Off road for 7.4km and turn left at the fork. In 6km, look for a narrow road on the left that goes down a short hill into a grassy area. There is a large mound of dirt in the middle marking the filled in coal mine.

Access #5 - Highway 16: From Prince George drive 55km east and turn left off Highway 16 into the Bowron River Recreational Site just before the Bowron River bridge.

Access #6 - Portage Canyon: Drive 15km east from the Willow River Bridge on Highway 16. Turn left on Vama Vama road and turn left again after approximately 40 metres. From this intersection, drive 6km to the put-in at the beginning of a BC Forest Recreation trail. Carry your boats approximately 400 metres down this steep and slippery trail to the river.

Access #7 - Lyle's Lawn: Drive 4km past the Portage Canyon put-in to a gravel pit on the right hand side of the road. Just before the gravel pit, turn right onto a narrow road. After 4km, you will reach the top of a hill that overlooks a clear cut. At the bottom of this hill, make a hard right turn; then in about 150 metres turn left. Lyle's lawn is 200-300m further along. Low clearance vehicles should not be used.

Access #8 - Box Canyon: Box Canyon is located on the Beaver Forest Road. This road can be accessed from Upper Fraser Road and from Highway 16. To access from the Upper Fraser Road, drive 17.5km from Prince George on Highway 16 east and turn left onto Upper Fraser Road. In 8km turn right onto the Beaver Forest Road and drive to kilometre 43 where the road crosses the Bowron. You can also access the Beaver Forest Road where Highway 16 crosses the Bowron River. Just after crossing the bridge, turn right, and right again at the T-junction. This is approximately kilometre 62 of the Beaver Forest Road.

Take-out – Hansard Bridge/Upper Fraser: Drive to Upper Fraser Road (see Access #8) past Upper Fraser to Hansard Bridge. This bridge is always staffed because it serves as both a train and vehicle bridge. The attendant may allow you to park in a small area on the east side of the bridge. Although not right on the river, a more secure place to leave your vehicle is near the Fire Hall just across the road from Upper Fraser sawmill. Ask the on site attendant where to park. If you choose to park at Upper Fraser, the take-out will be at the winter bridge site on river left just upstream of the sawmill.

Description: The Bowron River is very low in volume just downstream of its outflow from Bowron Lake, looking more like a large creek than a river. In the first 15km there are a fair number of log jams; most have passages through, but some may have to be portaged. The river meanders in this section and is Class 1 except for a short, easy Class 2 section just before Eighteen Mile Creek.

Ken Robinson

A typical log jam on the upper section

A boulder garden below the confluence with Indianpoint Creek also requires some manoeuvring. Approximately 11km above Haggen Creek, a 7km long canyon begins. At low to medium water levels, this canyon is Class 2+ and can be scouted from the water. Most of the canyon requires manoeuvering through boulders, but there is one drop towards the end that should be scouted. This drop can be run river left, but it would be fairly easy to line in medium to low water levels. At high water levels the canyon is rated as Class 3+. Lining may not be possible and portaging would be very difficult, so scout before running. If you choose to portage, expect a difficult climb up a steep bank to the road on river left (approximately 200 feet elevation gain). Just above Haggen Creek, log jams become evident again and are fairly common on corners and islands all the way downstream to the Fraser River.

Once Haggen Creek joins on the right, the river becomes medium volume. At low to medium water levels, the river is Class 1 to Tsus Creek (access #3). At higher water levels, the water flows faster and creates many riffles. Watch for log jams on corners and the upstream end of sandbars. Below Tsus Creek the water remains Class 1 for 13km. It is worth stopping at an old coal mine on river left 9km downstream from Tsus Creek. This old coal mine is a good take-out for people who do not want to paddle the boulder gardens before Highway 16.

Several short sections below the coal mine site contain boulders that require some maneouvering, but the most difficult boulder garden (Class 2+) begins approximately 3km before the Highway 16 Bridge and continues right to the bridge. It is marked by a slight increase in water velocity and a slight bend to the right; if you have topographic maps, two bends before the bridge. Scouting is difficult because of the length. The best way to run it is to continually eddy out behind boulders in the main stream and pick a route through.

Downstream of the Highway 16 Bridge, there are some boulders, pour-overs, surf waves, and holes. Stay left through Bear Canyon

Ken Robinson

The steep sloped canyon above Haggen Creek

because two ledges extend half way across the river from the right. Basket Canyon, 9km downstream of Highway 16, begins with a boulder garden and ends as a chute over a rocky outcrop. Watch for the log jam on river left at the chute. This can be a good play spot and is a nice location for lunch.

Wayne's World

Immediately across the river from the rest stop at the Highway 16 Bridge an excellent play spot can form in very high water. There is a small log jam on river left that water pours around, forming several foaming play waves called Wayne's World. With great surf and flat spinning opportunities, this can be an excellent park and play spot when the water is high enough in the spring.

For the next 5km, the river bends quite a bit, usually with rocky ledges protruding from the outside edge of each bend. The Class varies from 1 to 2. The river then straightens for 500m. At the end of the straight section, the river bends to the left past a large washed-out creek/mudslide and a big isolated boulder on river right - this is your warning that Portage Canyon is 500m downstream. Note, this is the most challenging portion of the river and is often run as a short play run by local paddlers. Refer to the Bowron River – Portage Canyon to Lyle's Lawn trip description for additional details.

In preparation for scouting or lining the canyon, stay on river right and eddy-out about 50m above the rocky ledge that will soon come into view. Portage Canyon is not really a canyon; the river bends gently to the left past a rocky ledge on the right and then plunges sharply right. There is a slight headwall on the left as the water piles into more rocky outcrops. Portage Canyon is Class 3 and should only be run by advanced paddlers in open boats and intermediate paddlers in closed boats. For those paddlers who choose to line, this can be done with some difficulty on the right. In high water lining is not an option and although not easy, the canyon can be portaged on river left.

Below the canyon there is a tricky rock garden with some tight manoeuvring to avoid boulders and hidden ledges. The river mellows for a while, passing through a few rock gardens before Boat

Canyon, which is more like a typical S-bend in the river. This can be scouted on the right. The rapid is Class is 2+.

The river slows into deep pools below this canyon and remains calm for another 5km after which it passes through a maze of log jams. The route through these log jams varies each year, so be prepared to scout and pull out of the river at any time. The most recent route through the maze of log jams is on river left after rounding a wide left bend at the start of the log jams. The channel does not look like much but do not be sucked into channels on the right, which merely end in impassable jams.

Once past the log jams the river bends sharply left through the vertical rock walls of Box Canyon. The entrance to the canyon has some tricky boils, but once in, at moderate water levels, the river is very mellow. At high water levels, there are big waves and boils in the canyon making it Class 2+. At the end of the canyon is the Beaver Forest Service Road Bridge; take out either on river left or on river right.

Barbara Robertson

Box Canyon has huge, steep, black canyon walls and little turbulence

The section from Box Canyon to the Fraser River is Class 1. The river slows, meanders a great deal and contains many log jams. The Bowron flows into the Fraser River 3km before the Hansard Bridge by Upper Fraser. There are no hazards on this stretch of the Fraser.

Camping: Organized campsites are located at the north end of Bowron Lake and at the Haggen Creek Forest Service Site. Between Bowron Lake and Haggen Creek there are very few camping spots because there are almost no gravel bars and very few possibilities on the riverbanks. There is one very nice site in a meadow by a hunting cabin a few hours above Indianpoint Creek, and although infrequently used, this land is probably privately owned. Camping is also possible at both bridge sites between Bowron Lake and Haggen Creek. Below Haggen Creek, many large gravel bars provide good campsites. A particularly nice site is at the confluence of Grizzly Creek, a few hours downstream of Haggen Creek. Between Haggen Creek and Highway 16 it is possible to camp at the old winter-bridge- crossing on river right just downstream of Tsus Creek (access #3) and at the old coalmine site (access #4) approximately 9km further downstream. Camping is not permitted at the recreation site at Highway 16. Downstream of Highway 16 camping is possible on gravel bars. A particularly nice place to stop is at the entrance to Box Canyon.

Bowron River - Portage Canyon to Lyle's Lawn

At a Glance: This medium volume river offers great surfing and hole playing and is a staple run for local paddlers. Fishing is also good and there are opportunities to view wildlife.

Best Time of Year: Surf waves and holes are best when the river has medium to high water levels. In spring, if the Willow River gauge reads 4 to 7 (see Getting There), water levels on the Bowron should be running at medium to high. Later in the season, this gauge is not as reliable an estimate. However, you can look at the boulders under the Highway 16 Bridge over the Bowron River (6.2km past the Vama Vama turn off); if the boulders upstream are just covered, paddling should be prime. See the water flow graph for the general Bowron River trip.

Maps: 93-G/16, Prince George Forest District Recreation Map

Rating: Class 3

Length: 8km

Time: 1 to 3 hours

Shuttle time: 15 minutes

Hazards:
•log jams at high water

Getting There: From Prince George, drive east on Highway 16 to the Willow River Bridge. You may want to have a quick look at the gauge here on the river left upstream side of the bridge. Drive 15km east of the Willow River Bridge, and look for the unmarked Vama Vama Forestry Road on your left.

Put-in: Turn left onto the Vama Vama Road, and then stay immediately left again, noting the mileage. From this intersection, drive 6km to the beginning of a BC Forest Recreation Trail; you should see a pullout on your right. Park here and carry your boats approximately 400m down a steep and often slippery trail to the river at Portage Canyon. From here you can avoid the canyon by carrying downstream. At very high levels, 7.0 or more on the Willow River gauge, it may not be possible to carry around the canyon drop.

Take-out: Continue past the put-in 3.7km to a small gravel pit on the right hand side of the road. Just before the gravel pit, turn right onto a narrow road. Travel down this road 4km, and you will reach the top of a hill that overlooks a clear-cut. At the bottom of this hill, make a hard right turn, and then about 150 metres in, turn left. Lyle's Lawn is 200m further along. Low clearance vehicles cannot travel this last 200m section. This take-out got its name after local paddler, Lyle Dickieson, who planted grass seed to make a great grass lawn at the take-out where there used to be nothing but mud!

Description: Before getting into your boat, scout Portage Canyon looking for logs and picking your line. This is the biggest rapid of the run, Class 3, and is generally run just river right of centre. River left tends to have a nasty hole that is best avoided. The two large eddies below can be used to pick up any swimmers or stray gear. Once the group is safely in one of the eddies, consider surfing the large, lively, breaking wave before heading downstream. After the canyon, the river continues for several kilometres with Class 2 to 2+ rapids and has many interspersed rocks for eddy practice, play holes, and surf waves.

Wayne Giles

The third wave at Wave Train with prime water levels

The next significant feature is Wave Train, a Class 3 rapid. To find this great surfing spot, look for the first cliff wall on river left. The river narrows somewhat to create large standing waves. Eddy out against the cliff wall on river left for excellent surfing opportunities. Surfing here is best when the spring levels on the Willow River gauge are near a 4. Note that any rescue should be quick here because swimmers could be carried through a hole just downstream. Below Wave Train is a short S-bend canyon and from this point, the river mellows, but there are a few play spots. To find the take-out, look for a giant house-sized rock on river right and a clear cut on the left bank. About 1km below this, the left bank drops to river level, and the right bank is steep and sandy. Look for flagging tape on river left and the short trail back to the vehicles at the take-out.

Camping: Unorganized at the take-out. Purden Lake Provincial Park, which offers a well-treed campground and a nice beach for swimming, is about a 15-minute drive further east on Highway 16.

James Taylor

Some of the local competitions include slalom events.

The Uncrafty Hovercraft

The waves of the rapids drowned the engine, turning the one-man hovercraft into an awkward barge. The clumsy craft flipped over on the next rock, trapping the lone occupant under the cockpit. The full force of the current caught the capsized hull and hurled it, clanging and banging, over the rocks and ledges through the powerful chutes of the grade 3 rapid.

Unable to escape, the man pinned under the hovercraft felt his legs break against the rocks. He struggled to remove his chest-high waders. At last, one final, desperate effort and the current ripped the waders away, allowing him to bob free. The swamped boat caught on the rocks mid-river and the exhausted survivor crawled onto the overturned hull.

Now what? Alone, midstream, in the Bowron River's Portage Canyon, far from the nearest road, things didn't look good at all. Prospects of swimming with more rapids downstream looked very unpleasant, but that would have to be attempted eventually. Ten long minutes passed. Then thirty minutes; an hour, an hour and a half. No point staying here. In another half hour, he would risk swimming.

Brightly coloured helmets and lifejackets bounced into view upstream. Five canoes rounded the corner and quickly descended. Five recreational paddlers from the Northwest Brigade Canoe Club, out to challenge the rapids in solo whitewater canoes gave the victim a future.

One paddler plucked the victim from his perched and ferried him to shore atop the airbags of his Mad River Canoe. Wet blue jeans were cut away from painful legs, soaked clothing was exchanged for dry garments and space blankets. Food and drink were provided. Two paddlers scouted an emergency evacuation route while another improvised splints from canoe paddles and triangular bandages.

The returning scouts advised that there would be no possibility of evacuation by land as the canyon was too steep (this was before the days of the Portage Canyon trail). Helicopter rescue might be possible but would be extremely difficult, if not dangerous and would take many hours to arrange. They decided to paddle the victim out in the bow of a Piranha canoe. Air bags were partly deflated to make room and both legs were splinted together. Meanwhile, tow ropes were rigged and with all five paddlers heaving on lines, they dragged the $9000 wreck off the rock, and winched it to shore for later salvage.

Paddling out was hazardous. The Piranha wasn't designed for dead weight in the bow. Swimming would have been next to impossible for the helpless victim. Extreme safety precautions were taken. Ten kilometers of river and three more rapids were negotiated before reaching Box Canyon.

The victim got a canoe ride he will never forget. Flanked by two rescue boats, with leader and sweep boats carefully picking the best course, the casualty felt secure enough to actually enjoy some parts of the two hour trip. Compared to his previous perch, this was positively relaxing.
At Box Canyon, the Piranha became a stretcher. In the station wagon, airbags were packed around the human cargo for transport to hospital. Luckily, only one leg was broken but the other was badly sprained. Six weeks in a cast healed the injuries and the hovercraft was floated out by a professional rafting crew..

Canoe River - Water Gauge to Highway 5

At a Glance: An exciting medium volume mountain river with great scenery and plenty of exciting drops. This run is continuous white-water from start to finish. Down to where the power line crosses, it is steady downstream running with small eddies. From the power line on, you get into the ledge section. The bottom section is quite pushy.

Best Time of Year: Anytime it is open. When it is low, there are play spots; when high, it is fast and furious. High water is at run off, after several hot days, or after a heavy rain.

Hazards: River level fluctuates quickly with rain and warmer weather. The water is always extremely cold so wear appropriate cold water gear even on a hot summer day.

Maps: 83-D/11, 83-D/14, Robson Valley Forest District Recreation Map

Getting There: From Prince George, travel east on Highway 16 to the junction of Highway 5. Take Highway 5 south to Valemount. From 5th Ave. in Valemount, continue south on Highway 5 approximately 5km to Kinbasket Lake Road on the right

Take-out: Continue on Highway 5 past the Kinbasket Lake Road turnoff for approximately 2km to the bridge over the Canoe River. The take-out is on the downstream, south side of the bridge.

Rating: Class 3+ to 4-

Length: 12km

Time: 3 hours

Shuttle time: 15 minutes

Hazards:
•fluctuating water levels
•cold water

Put-in: Return to Kinbasket Lake Road. Turn off onto Kinbasket Lake Road and follow it for 1km to a fork in the road. Take the left fork onto West Ridge Forest Service Road, and continue for 5.5km to an old bridge on the left at the Canoe River. This is a possible take-out or put-in location if you wish to shorten the trip or avoid the ledge section. Drive another 6.7km down the West Ridge Forest Service Road to a small cart track on the left. Watch carefully for this trail. Walk down the trail for 200m to the river at the water gauge station.

Description: The put-in is an easy carry down to the river at the water gauging station. The first kilometre of the river is a gentle warm-up with large eddies, easy holes, and waves. The river then picks up, dropping continuously downhill for the next 8km. About every kilometre, there is an eddy large enough for boats to gather in. Otherwise, it is continuous Class 3+ whitewater requiring the paddler to dodge holes, paddle through boiling hydraulics, and if desired, catch waves on the fly. A swim here would not be fun or recommended as it would be a long abrasive swim through very cold water. Extended time in the water is very hazardous.

When the river flattens out a bit, you will see a broad horizon line and know that there is a big drop coming, Class 3+. This 2 to 3m drop is right under the power lines and should be scouted. The next drop is Headwall, a Class 4 rapid not far below "Powerline." If unfamiliar with the river, this drop should be scouted from river left. There are four or five ledge drops below Powerline in the last 3km. There is good play throughout this section rated as Class 3+ to 4. As you would expect, the higher the level, the more intense the action is. Scouting is difficult. If in doubt, go where the main flow goes. The section ends in a scenic canyon before widening out down to the take-out.

Camping: Good camping is available on the river 4km upstream of the put-in at the Forest Recreation Site. Good camping is also available in Valemount or, better yet, at Mount Robson. If you have a group, try to get the group campsite as it has the best view.

Cariboo River

The Cariboo River is a medium volume river. Watch the beautiful rounded rocks on the bottom flow quickly by or pause and look for fish in the deep pools. The river offers two great white water paddling trips. Advanced paddlers will enjoy a run down the upper section while intermediate paddlers and beginners (with an intermediate paddlers' leadership) will be entertained on the lower section.

Wayne Giles

The Michelin Man doesn't need floatation for his boat!

Cariboo River - Upper

At a Glance: The Cariboo River offers easily accessible whitewater paddling for advanced/expert paddlers on beautiful clear water in a wilderness setting.

Best Time of Year: May to October. Paddling the river in flood is not recommended; eddies become non-existent and scouting not possible.

Maps: 93-A/11, 93-A/12, Cariboo Forest Region Recreation Map (East)

Getting There: From Prince George, drive 188km south on Highway 97 to the town of McLeese Lake. When entering town adjacent to the lake, turn left onto Beaver Lake Road at the signs indicating Gibraltar Mines and Likely. Follow this road for 3km climbing a steep hill, and then veer right just past the power lines, following the signs to Likely and Horsefly. Follow Beaver Lake Road (gravel) for approximately 30km to its end at the road leading to Likely. Turn left at the highway and follow it for approximately 35km to the town of Likely.

Rating: Class 4 to 4+

Length: 10km

Time: 2.5 hours

Shuttle time: 15 minutes

Hazards:
- snags
- wood in river

Take-out: Cross the bridge in Likely and continue north on Keithley Creek Road, which turns from pavement to gravel. Approximately 7km from Likely, the road crosses the Cariboo River. Take out using the very steep trail on river right, upstream of the bridge.

Alternate Take-out: An easier take-out exists about 1km downstream from the bridge. Take the first left after the bridge onto Pearson Road. Continue a short distance and look for a spur road on the left heading down to the river. Follow this road a short distance and turn left again follow a small cart track about 200m to an obvious beach access and parking area.

Put-in: Continue on the Keithley Creek Road past the bridge over the Cariboo River at the take-out. At the 15km sign, turn right onto an old logging road and continue through a cut-block for a short distance. As the road comes closer to the river, it turns left and heads up-stream to the fish ladder at Cariboo River Falls. At this point, you will most likely encounter a locked gate. If the gate is locked, you have a short walk on a good road to the river access. Continue until you see a rock cairn or trail sign on your right. At this point, a trail descends to the river, below the falls, for a safe put-in. If you go too far, you will encounter the fish channel at the base of the falls. There is a gauge system on the rocks at the put-in. Higher water levels are considered 4 and up.

Description: The upper section of the Cariboo River passes through several historic sites associated with the Cariboo Gold Rush such as Seller Creek and Murderer Creek. Around most bends in the river, there are signs of old and new placer mining workings and the occasional derelict cabin.

The put-in is located just below the Class 5 Cariboo River Falls. The upper portion (approximately 2km) of the river is the most difficult section containing several Class 4 rapids interspersed with Class 3. Below this the river is mostly class two until the Class 3 rapid just before the bridge at the takeout.

The run starts below the falls with a set of Class 3 rapids. The river then flattens and you encounter Bubbleyum: two Class 4 rapids containing large waves and holes. The first portion of the rapid is best run starting slightly left of centre. There is a short pool at the bottom to pick up swimmers. After a brief respite, the next series of Class 3 rapids is the McGirrgitater with 2 big holes in the center of the river and good surfing on the lower section. The next rapid, Best Western, is located about 2km down river in an S-bend; look for an old cabin on the north shore, river right. The final set of rapids before the bridge, Fluffy Bunny, is Class 3. Take-out at the Keithley Creek Road Bridge or beach 1km downstream, depending on which take-out is chosen.

Camping: At the town of Likely or at Quesnel Forks.

Cariboo River - Lower

At a Glance: This stretch of the Cariboo River offers easily accessible whitewater for intermediate paddlers with superb camping at the take-out.

Best Time of Year: May to October

Maps: 93-A/12, Cariboo Forest Region Recreation Map (East). An excellent description and map of this trip is available at www.imagehouse.com/guidemaps/home.htm

Getting There: From Prince George, drive 188km south on Highway 97 to the town of McLeese Lake. When entering town adjacent to the lake turn left onto Beaver Lake Road at the signs indicating Gibraltar Mines and Likely. Follow this road for 3km climbing a steep hill and then veer right just past the power lines following the signs to Likely and Horsefly. Follow Beaver Lake Road (gravel) for approximately 30km to its end at the road leading to Likely. Turn left at the highway and follow it for approximately 35km to the town of Likely.

Rating: Class 2 to 3

Length: 12km

Time: 3 hours

Shuttle time: 25 minutes

Hazards:
•snags
•wood in river

Take-out: A well maintained forestry road services the historic site of Quesnel Forks, the location of the take-out. It is about 15km from the bridge in Likely. After crossing the bridge continue up the hill. Turn left at the first opportunity and follow the signs to Quesnel Forks. Stay left at all junctions. The best take-out is now just past the old cemetery. There has been tremendous erosion at the lower take-out over the past couple years due to a huge landslide just upstream.

Put-in: Return to Likely turning left at Likely continuing through town on the main road out of town (north) as it turns from pavement to gravel (keep going on the road over the bridge). Approximately 7km from Likely the road crosses the Cariboo River. Put in using the very steep trail on river right, upstream of the bridge.

Alternate Put-in: An easier put-in exists about 1 to 2km downstream from the bridge. Take the first left after the bridge onto Pearson Road. Continue a short distance and look for a spur road heading down to the river (about 200m) to an obvious beach access and parking area.

Description: The lower section of the Cariboo River should be considered Class 2 to 3, 3 in higher water. Run centre throughout this section. Look for frequent boulders and standing waves with steep banks on the outside of bends. About 2km from the bridge, the river goes through a narrow canyon with big standing waves. The next rapid occurs at 3km from the bridge where the river passes over a ledge. At low water, the lower section is suitable for open boats and beginner kayakers with intermediate guidance. High water requires advanced skills. The recommended take-out is at the old ghost town of Quesnel Forks. If canoe tripping, it is possible to continue downstream on the Quesnel River (see the Quesnel River trip report).

Camping: The site of Quesnel Forks, located at the confluence of the Cariboo and Quesnel Rivers, is a designated B.C. Forestry campground. Camping at this popular location is excellent on the site of this historic gold mining city. Campers and souvenir seekers have looted the town for artifacts and scavenged pieces of the buildings for firewood. Please respect this site and leave it as you found it.

Camping: At the town of Likely or at Quesnel Forks.

Quesnel Forks - Historical Note[1]

In 1859, miners tracing gold up the Quesnel River stopped to work the gravel delta at the junction of the North and South Forks, now called the Cariboo and Quesnel Rivers. The village that quickly formed could soon boast the largest population north of San Francisco (until Barkerville eclipsed its glory with the gold strike of 1862). A number of entrepreneurs quickly applied for a toll bridge charter to connect the rapidly growing village with the trail to the Fraser River. Sam Alder and William Berry won out and their bridge was in place by 1862, in time to serve the hordes of miners and the pack trains that came through that summer on their way to the gold fields.

From the very beginning, government officials were dubious about the future of the village. In his report to Governor James Douglas in 1860, Gold Commissioner Philip Henry Nind thought the town should be moved. There should be a better location "...than a flat lying between two swift rivers which can only be approached by terrific hills, is many miles distant from pasture, and ....where no money or labour can ever make even a moderately good road."

Quesnel Forks was beset by its share of problems over the years. On the morning of October 12, 1880, fire consumed most of the earliest buildings. Two more fires in the 1880's did considerable damage to the commercial buildings. But the residents persevered. The vibrant Chinese community was responsible for much of the rebuilding. If the 1881 Canada Census is correct, then the Keithly Creek/Quesnel Forks census area had the third largest concentration of Chinese residents, after Victoria and Nanaimo. Because Quesnel Forks was the supply centre for more than 250 Chinese miners and farmers, many of these cabins, stores, and warehouses were rebuilt after the fires.

The peaceful routines in the little village were again badly shaken in the early 1890's, when corporate businessmen invested thousands of dollars in the placer mines, creating a hydraulic mining boom. Executives of the Canadian Pacific Railway hired John Hobson, a mining engineer from

1 Information taken from the Friends of Barkerville Historical Society website.

California, to supervise development of the Bullion Pit Mine. By 1900 this mine was described as one of the largest open pit mines in the Commonwealth. Despite miles of ditches and pipelines, and the damming of numerous lakes, there was never enough water to operate for more than several months. Nevertheless, the mine produced $350,000 in 1900, putting the Quesnel Mining section ahead of the Barkerville section in gold production.

Mining at the Bullion Pit continued until June 1907 when it was shut down. Quesnel Forks went into decline, reviving slightly in the 1930's when the mine reopened. But it never matched the activity of the 1890's, and after World War II the village attracted only a few hardy miners. In 1948, the year of the great Fraser River floods, the South Fork Bridge was washed out and never replaced. A new road built in the 1930's through Likely and Cedar Creek, using a bridge at the Quesnel dam site, also helped to put Quesnel Forks in a backwater.

In recent years, the Likely Cemetery Society has restored many of the graves in the historic cemetery. Here you will find markers for the pioneers who made Quesnel Forks a special community, including William Berry, the toll bridge owner, William and Jennie Stephenson, and their son Gillespie, and more than twenty Chinese men and women. Recently, the Friends of Barkerville Historical Society took on the protection of the buildings and the site as a major project. The society sees their involvement at Quesnel Forks including the encouragement and assistance in the preservation of its unique historic resource and the provision of information to the public to enhance their appreciation of the site's significance.

Wandering among the old cabins, or along the riverbank near the toll bridge site, it is difficult to believe that in twenty years the ghost town of Quesnel Forks will disappear forever. After more than one hundred years of fighting the elements, according to heritage experts, the fragile buildings cannot hold up much longer, and yet one wishes Quesnel Forks could be frozen in time.

Carp Lake

At a Glance: Carp Lake is interesting to explore because of its many coves, bays, and islands. It is located on the Nechako Plateau and surrounded by forests of spruce, pine, and aspen. Wildlife is abundant and moose can often be seen foraging in marshy areas along the lakeshore. Excellent fishing attracts many people; however, rustic campsites on out-of-the-way islands provide a true wilderness experience.

Maps: 93-J/14, Prince George District Recreation Map. More detailed maps and information contact BC Parks Prince George Office, Box 2045 (4051 18th Ave.), Prince George, BC, V2N 2J6. Telephone: (250) 565-6340.

Getting there: From Prince George, take Highway 97 to the north end of McLeod Lake (141km). Turn left (west) and drive 32km to Carp Lake Campground.

Length:14km north to south

Time: 1 to 4 days

Hazards:
- unpredictable shallows
- high winds

Best time: spring to fall

Description: The only road access to Carp Lake is from the main campsite at Kettle Bay. Before canoeing, you may enjoy walking some of the park trails. The trail to War Falls is especially interesting. After launching, watch for sandy beaches on the right, the first just as you leave Kettle Bay, and the second a kilometre further along. The water at the second beach stays shallow for a long distance and makes a great swimming spot for small children. The south side of the lake has a number of smooth rock beaches. Moose, bear, and deer are seen fairly often as are ducks and geese during spring and fall. Loons, of course, are common any time you visit.

Camping: There is a large provincial campsite at Kettle Bay that can be reserved ahead of time if you choose. From this campsite, you can paddle to any of the four island campsites within a few hours. Be sure to pick up a Carp Lake Provincial Park brochure, which marks the location of these sites.

The Bear Facts

Summer '91 on the Willow River. Nice day for a paddle. A group of paddlers invite along a special guest from South Africa. She accepts. She'd like to watch a bunch of boaters playing on the river.

They gather on the Willow River Bridge for the usual pre-run level check. They direct their guest to walk up the path to surf city. Alone. She looks a little worried. She asks about bears. (After all, in her country, there are many dangerous things in the wild.) They reassure her. "Haven't seen a bear in these here parts since the summer of '42."

No problem. She walks. She watches. She swats flies. Fun!

The next night, another group heads out on the same river. Playing on the wave below the cutbank, they hear a noise. Looking upstream they see - a grizzly sow charging down the bank straight towards them! Whoooeeee!

Wayne Giles

Setting up to take advantage of the high winds often on the lake.

10 Chilako River (Mud River)

At a Glance: A good beginner run very close to town, this is a popular run very early in the season when other rivers are still frozen.

Best Time of Year: spring, in high and medium water levels, which are generally anywhere from 8 to 13 boards on the gauge (see Getting There). 11 boards is the ideal level.

Maps: 93-G/5, Prince George Forest District Recreation Map

Getting There: Drive west on Highway 16 for 16km, passing the community of Beaverly, to the Mud River Valley. At the bottom on the hill descending into the valley, turn right onto Lower Mud River Road. Follow this road for 2.5km to the bridge over the Mud River. Stop here and check the gauge. Local paddlers gauge this river by counting how many boards are showing above waterline.

Rating: Class 2

Length: 5km

Time: 1 hour

Shuttle time: 10 minutes

Hazards:
- logs
- log jams
- sweepers

Put-in: Continuing over the bridge, the road turns to gravel in 2.5km. Follow the gravel road for 1km and then take the smaller gravel road on the right, Chilako Station Road. Follow this road for 1.4km to another small road on the right leading down to a private property. Follow this road for 300m. Park at the river just before the house making sure you do not block the access.

Take-out: Drive back out of the put-in road and turn right (continuing on Chilako Station Road). Drive for 1.3km to where the road ends at a T-junction. The road to the right is Olinger Road and the road straight ahead is posted `No Through Road'. Take the driveway leading straight ahead and proceed down the hill. You will see a small road on the right at the bottom of the hill. Park here and do not proceed down this road. The property owner has been kind enough to let us use this access but does not want anyone driving down this road as it is often too muddy. You will have to walk 500m up this road from the river to your vehicle.

Description: This is a low volume river that is ideal for the beginner, with intermediate accompaniment, or intermediate, who wants to brush up on paddling skills. It is also a good evening run for those who live in Prince George.

There are a few good surf waves on the run down and the odd boulder garden requiring some manoeuvring. Look for the Dead-Dog Rapid where the river is pushed up against some clay cliffs on river left. These rapids are not as bad as they may sound, merely some larger standing waves to negotiate through.

You will pass two large cut-banks located on river left as the river bends right. If they are still snow-covered, try your luck hauling your boat up one of these cut-banks and seal launching into the river. If you try this when the snow is gone, you will see where the river gets its nickname! The take-out is on river left just past the second set of cut-banks. There is a level field on the shore.

Note: Other sections of the river can be paddled, but they are generally choked with many beaver dams and some log jams. The section past the take-out can be run down to the Nechako River, which is about 1km downstream. There are several takeouts on the Nechako between here and Prince George.

Camping: during lower water levels gravel bars provide plenty of camping opportunities.

Barbara Robertson

Climbing up the snow banks (also note mud) for a fast ride!

Chilako Clearcut

The Mud River was overgrown with sweepers and jams. It was ripe for cleaning. A frightening group of maniacs with assorted axes and saws met and proceeded to slash and hack their way down the run. The water was low, so their canoes bumped along the gravel bottom, sustaining only minor damage.

Paul felt that standing in a canoe chainsawing a log jam was boring, especially since he was strictly prohibited from cutting into the gunwale. The canoe filled with sawdust. Glen felled a tree across the canoe. Paul fell into a log jam, catching his eyeglasses on the end of a springy willow. The glasses flew into space. Paul's world grew murky. The others found him crawling among the sticks, face close to the ground, hunting for his glasses. Soon, ten helpers were also worming around the log jam muttering, "They must have gone into the river." They began pulling the log jam apart, piece by piece, and tossing it over Melissa's head into the river. Melissa stood in the water, peering into its muddy depths, cringing from all the flying debris.

Finally, Phil advised Paul to announce that they were giving up. He explained that the glasses would only be found after abandoning the search. Paul, in his usual good humour, said, "Alright, I give up!" Instantly, Melissa screamed from the river, "I found them!"

Barbara Robertson

Surfing made easy with the anchor out!

Chilcotin River (Hanceville to Durell Ranch)

At a Glance: A scenic day trip through the beautiful Chilcotin countryside on a mostly flat river interspersed with some fun, up to Class 3, rapids. The river runs through several canyons and is contained in a steep-walled valley for its entire length.

Best Time of Year: during low water, in early spring or late summer. The river tends to reach flood levels in the summer.

Maps: 92-O/14, 92-O/15, Cariboo Forest Region Recreation Map (West)

Getting There: From Prince George, drive south on Highway 97 to Williams Lake. Travel west from Williams Lake on Highway 20 for approximately one hour to Lees Corner (Hanceville).

Put-in: Turn left off Highway 20 at Lees Corner (the Hanceville Post Office) and travel 3km to the Chilcotin River Bridge; put in here.

Rating:
Class 2 to 3 in lower water

Length: 33km

Time: 8 hours

Shuttle time: 40 minutes

Hazards:
•snags
•wood in river

Take-out: Approximately 25km east of Hanceville (or 16km west of the small community of Riske Creek), there is a sign on the south side of Highway 20 saying “16k Wine Glass Durrells.” Turn down the narrow dirt road and drive for 16km to the Wine Glass Ranch located beside the Chilcotin River. The last portion of the road is very narrow and steep. Be sure to ask permission from Brian and Jane Durrell and make sure to leave all gates open or closed as you found them.

Description: The river starts gently from the open valley, but then drops into Hanceville Canyon marked by cliffs on the left side and Class 2+ drops. Watch for a short scramble up to a bat cave above the river on the left. After a series of delightful rapids in the canyon, there is a 20km flat section leading up to Big Creek Canyon. After you enter Big Creek Canyon and just after Big Creek flows in on the right, you reach Big Creek Rapids, Class 3. Pull out on river right to scout the rapids. Big Creek Rapids consist of big, pushy standing waves leading into a boulder garden. Shortly after these rapids, you will reach the take-out on river left at the Wine Glass Ranch. Although not paddled downstream of this point by our club, with research, this trip could be significantly extended down river.

Camping: There is good, organized camping available at the Forestry Recreation Site just west of Riske Creek. Also, there is an excellent campsite at Bull Canyon on the Chilcotin River 9km west of Alexis Creek and left down from Highway 20.

Chilko River – Chilko Lake to Bull Canyon (Chilcotin River)

At a Glance: The Chilko River offers the best wilderness white water paddling in the Williams Lake region with extensive Class 3 rapids and some Class 4+. The Chilko is host to commercial rafting trips and is well known for its fly fishing nearer Chilko Lake. There is also a very nice option for a canoeing day trip starting from Chilko Lake.

The river is most widely paddled by experienced whitewater boaters who want the excitement and play that the section from the Kayak put-in to the Taseko River Junction offers. However, intermediate canoeists will also enjoy the day tripping section from Chilko Lake to the Raft Put-in. More advanced canoeists might also consider the section from the Raft put-in to the Kayak put-in and from Taseko Junction to Bull Canyon

Rating: Class 4+

Length: 9 to 33km depending on section

Time: 1.5 to 6 hours depending on section

Shuttle time: 0.5 to 2 hours depending on section

Hazards:
•very technical
•snags

Best time: May to October

Length: Approximate lengths of each section are shown below.
Chilko Lake to Raft Put-in: 33km
Raft Put-in to Kayak Put-in: 11 km
Kayak Put-in to Eagle's Claw: 9 km
Eagle's Claw to Taseko Junction: 13km
Taseko Junction to Bull Canyon: 27km

Time:
Chilko Lake to Raft Put-in: 4 hours
Raft Put-in to Kayak Put-in: 1.5 hour
Kayak Put-in to Eagle's Claw: 2 hours
Eagle's Claw to Taseko Junction: 2 hours
Taseko Junction to Bull Canyon (Chilcotin River): 6 hours

Shuttle Time: Allow 30 minutes to drive between the access points of each section described; the road is very rough and slow going. Allow two hours to drive from Bull Canyon to Chilko Lake.

Hazards: This is a very technical river; run the river with someone who is familiar with it. You are strongly advised to scout frequently along the river before descending. Watch for snags or wood in the river. There is an extreme hazard at Siwash Bridge on the section below Taseko River Junction down to Bull Canyon – avoid at high water.

Maps: 92-N/6, 92-N/9, 92O/13, 93-B/4, Cariboo Forest Region Recreation Map (West)

Getting There: From Prince George, drive south on Highway 97 to Williams Lake. Travel west from Williams Lake on Highway 20 for approximately 112km to Alexis Creek.

Take-out: Bull Canyon
Continue on Highway 20 West for another 6km to Bull Canyon Provincial Park. This is the take-out if you choose to paddle the complete Chilko River and a short portion of the Chilcotin River.

Access #1: Taseko River Junction Forest Service Site
Continue another 13km past Bull Canyon (19 km past Alexis Creek) and turn left (south) onto the Chilko-Newton Road veering immediately to the right. Set your odometre to zero here. Travel for 1.5 km to where the road heads to the left (onto the 7000 Road) and where you cross a small bridge. At kilometer 4.5 on the 7000 Road, turn right. A small sign post indicates Chilko Station. (Note: If you continue straight you will cross the Chilko River on the Siwash Bridge. You should scout this bridge on the way up if you are running the section down to Bull Canyon. See the hazards section). This small road (Chilko-Newton Road) continues south, running more or less parallel to the Chilko River, eventually reaching the headwaters in Chilko Lake.

You will travel over a cattle-guard at 5.5 km and 11.5 km, measured from odometer zero at the highway. Taseko River Junction Forest Service Site is located on the right 17km from odometre zero. This is the most common take-out location for whitewater kayak trips.

Access #2: Kayak Put-in

To reach the most common kayak put-in, continue on the Chilko-Newton Road for 30 to 40 minutes driving time. The road climbs a series of switchbacks and then meets the river at a cutbank high above the river. This is the first place the river and access road meet when driving upstream. There is a pull-out on the left, this the Kayak put-in. To put-in, scramble down the hill to the river. Note that there is also a possible put-in at Eagle's Claw that is reached prior to the kayak put-in, however, its exact location is unknown to the authors.

Access #3 and #4: Raft Put-in and Henry's Crossing

Continue south from the kayak put-in on the Chilko-Newton Road to the Raft put-in (you will see a ramp down to the river on your left and an area for camping). After the Raft put-in you will continue straight ahead but encounter a road heading to the right to Tatla Lake. Henry's Crossing is located just past this junction, there is a bridge over the Chilko River.

Put-in: Chilko Lake

If you continue south on the Chilko-Newton Road past Henry's Crossing you will finally reach Chilko Lake. Check at the lodge for permission to launch or park, or find a site on Crown Land further north.

Ian Norn

Commercial rafting outfitters offer trips on the Chilko River.

Description: The following description begins with a put-in at Chilko Lake Lodge (the beginning of the river). The section descriptions are based on the most commonly used put-in/take-out locations.

Chilko Lake to the Raft Put-in

The river begins as easy Class 1 to 2 with no real rapids or hazards. You float past two major access points, Henry's Crossing and a commercial raft campsite on the left (look for a major ramp down to the river). Canoes should take out here. Up to this point the Chilko is wide, not fast, and provides beautiful views of the surrounding mountains and forests in Tyslo's Provincial Park and beyond, making for a wonderful canoeing day trip.

Graham Gerry

The Chilko has many stretches of continuous, cold, whitewater.

Raft Put-in to Kayak Put-in

Once beyond the river raft campsite, the river begins to take on more canyon features with small rapids up to Class 3 and some big waves at high water. Watch for wood hazards. You approach the most common kayak put-in on river left where there is a steep slope down to the river. It is a short, steep climb out should you choose to use this as a take-out.

Kayak Put-in to Eagle's Claw

Here the river really picks up pace. The Chilko passes through basalt formations and becomes steeper with more rocks in the drops and frequent holes. The surfing picks up and provides a ton of play. Once it starts to get really big, you have reached the infamous Bidwell rapid. You can recognize this drop as the river bends right and drops at a very impressive gradient. Eddy out on river left to scout. There is a short trail up to a vantage point giving you a view of the drop. Watch for hidden wood, usually at bottom left.

After Bidwell comes more play and the legendary White Mile (known for a movie), one kilometre of huge continuous waves interspersed with holes. This rapid ends with a hard right turn and then mellows until the Eagle's Claw. Eagle's Claw is a Class 4 rapid with many large boulders and very aerated water. The rapid can be scouted on the drive up to the put-in. Take out at Eagle's Claw to avoid the easier, flat last 10km. The Eagle's Claw would also be a good put-in for intermediate paddlers. The put-in is at the bottom of the rapid.

Eagle's Claw to Taseko River Junction

After about 15 minutes of paddling downstream from Eagle's Claw (see above), you enter Lava Canyon with its spectacular 30ft vertical black basalt walls. The water in the canyon is flat though quite swirly. The small caves in the canyon walls offer some unique locations to practice your eddy turns!

Downstream, the only challenge is Maytag, a Class 3+ S-bend rapid with a hole, located approximately 2km below Lava Canyon. After this rapid, the river is flat with braided channels continuing to the Taseko River junction and the take-out for whitewater kayak trips.

Taseko River Junction to Bull Canyon

This portion of the trip is mostly on the Chilcotin River and is Class 2 to 3. This is generally a fun, playful run with amazing beauty and lots of surf. Watch for wood at midstream where the Chilko joins the Chilcotin River. The most hazardous spot on this section is at Siwash Bridge where there can be a big re-circulating hydraulic.

Warning: the river funnels into a narrow opening about 4 metres wide between the bridge piers. It is essential to scout this and it should be avoided at high water.

Camping: The Taseko River Junction Ministry of Forests Recreation Site along the Chilko River on the Chilko-Newton Road is the preferred site for whitewater kayakers (see Getting There) though many other forest recreation sites exist in the area. Camping is also available at Chilko Lake and at Bull Canyon Provincial Park on the Chilcotin River along Highway 20.

Sean Fraser

Bidwell Canyon at low water.

Clearwater and Azure Lakes

At a Glance: Located in the mountains of Wells Gray Provincial Park, these two long lakes are joined by a short portage and offer wonderful wilderness camping with sandy beaches. Although powerboats can access both lakes, the size of the lakes keeps things quiet and the scenery and campsites make it a very worthwhile trip.

Length:	Clearwater Lake	21km
	Azure Lake	24km
	river connector	3km, includes a 500m portage trail

Maps: 93-A/1, 93-A/8, 83-D/5, Kamloops Forest Region Recreation Map, Clearwater Forest District Recreation Map. Also, stop at the visitor centre at the junction of Highway 5 and Clearwater Valley Road to check on a park permit, maps of the park, and road, weather and camping conditions in the park. Contact the centre at:

Wells Gray Information Centre
Box 1988, RR1
Clearwater B.C. V0E 1N0
Tel: (250) 674-2646

Camping reservations can be made by contacting the Discover Camping Campground Reservation Service at www.discover-camping.ca. Telephone: 1-800-689-9025.

Rating: Class 1

Length: 102km round trip

Time: 4 days

Hazards:
•high winds/waves
•waterfall at outlet of Clearwater lake
•must follow safe channel through river connector

Best time: June to October

Getting There: From Prince George, drive south on Highway 97 to Highway 24 East to Lone Butte and Little Fort. Follow Highway 24 to its end at Little Fort on Highway 5. Drive north on Highway 5 to the town of Clearwater following the signs leading to Wells Gray Provincial Park.

Alternatively, drive east on Highway 97 from Prince George and then south on Highway 5 to the town of Clearwater. Driving time and distances are very comparable to the directions given above.

Near Clearwater you will see signs directing you to Wells Gray Provincial Park. Follow the signs down the Wells Gray Park Road (Clearwater Valley Road), which is paved for the first 43kms. The park gate is located at Hemp Creek, 40km north on this road from Highway 5. From Hemp Creek follow the 28km of gravel road to Clearwater Lake. Put-in at either Clearwater Lake Campground or the nearby boat launch.

Description: Perhaps not as well known, and therefore not as busy as Murtle Lake, Clearwater and Azure Lakes offer many of the same experiences. The mountain scenery is beautiful and the campsites excellent. Be prepared to see powerboats on the lakes, but they are infrequent and do not detract significantly from the trip. Guided boat tours are available.

From the Clearwater Lake Campsite, the nicest paddling is up the east (right) shore of Clearwater Lake. Once at the Clearwater River leading to Azure Lake, again stay on the east shore to access the portage trail. Paddling up the river can be difficult depending on water levels. In lower water levels powerboats cannot navigate the river. Perhaps this is the best time to go! The portage trail is 500m long but climbs nearly 100 steps.

Paul Walsh

Sea kayaking is a popular option on Clearwater Lake

Paul Walsh

Great alpine hiking can be accessed from the lakes in several locations

Once on Azure Lake, make sure you don't miss the highlight of the lake: Rainbow Falls. Wildlife abounds in the swampy areas at the east end of Azure Lake. Another nice diversion is the Huntley Col Hiking Route, a long day hike with 1300m of elevation gain leading to the 2429m Mount Huntley. Allow a minimum of 8 hours. You can also do a full day hike into Hobson Lake and back (8 hours). This is a fairly easy 15km hike (300m elevation gain) leaving from the river between Clearwater and Azure Lakes. The Clearwater River into Hobson Lake is not navigable. Rental canoes are available for use on the lake. Check at the information centre for additional information.

Camping: There are 12 designated campsites on Clearwater and Azure Lakes. On Clearwater Lake the campsite at Ivory Creek is designated as canoeist only. Osprey Campsite on Azure Lake is reserved for canoeists only (located immediately across from the Huntley Col Hiking Route). You must have a park camping permit obtained at the self-registration system at the boat launch.

14 Clearwater River

This beautiful river is a favourite for B.C. rafters and experienced kayakers. There are three separate sections that can be run as day trips starting with the Upper section located where the Clearwater River exits Clearwater Lake in Wells Gray Provincial Park. The other two runs, the Middle and Lower sections, are accessed from the west side of the river. The most common kayak and rafting run is the Lower section. For novice and intermediate paddlers there is a good park and play wave in the Middle section.

Paul Berry

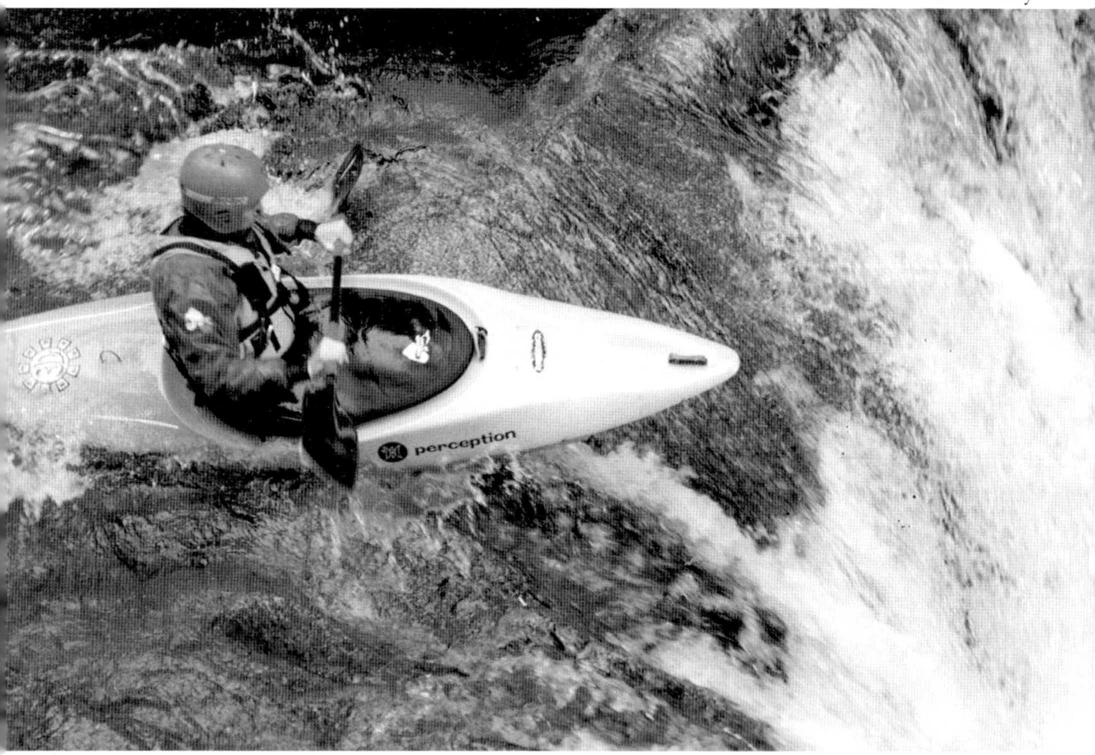

At the brink of one of the runnable falls.

Clearwater River – Upper

At a Glance: This run is a very difficult section of the river with numerous waterfalls as well as significant sustained difficult rapids. Paddle with someone who has run the river and is familiar with its features, and paddle with extreme caution. If you are up for the paddle, the Clearwater is spectacular with lots of play, adrenaline-pumping rapids, and great scenery.

Best Time of Year: usually August or September when the water levels are between 1 to 3 on the gauge. The gauge is found on the first cement bridge on the Old North Thompson Highway Road heading upstream (the bridge in town). The river gauge can be seen on the south upstream side of the bridge.

Maps: 92-P/9, 92-P/16. Kamloops Forest Region Recreation Map, Clearwater Forest District Recreation Map.

Rating: Class 4 to 5

Length: 6km

Time: 3 to 4 hours

Shuttle time: 10 minutes

Hazards: Bailey' s Chute and Donkey Falls must be portaged

Also, stop at the visitor centre at the junction of Highway 5 and Clearwater Valley Road to check on a park permit, maps of the park, and road, weather and camping conditions in the park. Contact the centre at:

Wells Gray Information Centre
Box 1988, RR1
Clearwater B.C. V0E 1N0
Tel: (250) 674-2646

Getting There: From Prince George, drive south on Highway 97 to Highway 24 East to Lone Butte and Little Fort. Follow Highway 24 to its end at Little Fort on Highway 5. Drive north on Highway 5 to the town of Clearwater, following the signs leading to Wells Gray Provincial Park.

Alternately, drive east on Highway 97 from Prince George and then south on Highway 5 to the town of Clearwater. Driving time and distances are very comparable to the directions given above.

Take-out – Bailey's Chute: at the river trail to Bailey's Chute. Near Clearwater, you will see signs directing you to Wells Gray Provincial Park. Follow the signs up the Wells Gray Park Road (Clearwater Valley Road) of which the first 43kms are paved. The park gate is located at Hemp Creek, 40km north on this road from Highway 5. From Hemp Creek, drive another 15km to the river trail leading to Bailey's Chute.

Put-in – Clearwater Lake: Continue north on the Wells Gray Park Road to Clearwater Lake, a distance of approximately 6km. The put-in is located at the Clearwater Lake Campground near the falls. This put-in location places you above an 8-10 foot waterfall that drops into the Clearwater River.

Alternate Put-in – Falls Creek Waterfall: Just downstream of the put-in described above.

Description: The waterfalls at the put-in can be portaged on a good trail. Scout the falls before putting the boats in the water. After Falls Creek Waterfall, the river is Class 1 to 2 for approximately 1km. You will then see a house-sized rock located on river left; watch here for a big, green surf wave. Further downstream, you enter a very active Class 3 to 3+ canyon that is approximately 1.5 to 2km long; avoid a nasty hole on river left. At the bottom of the last drop, paddle on river right a short distance (less than 1km) and take out to scout the next Class 4 drop. Below this drop, the next large feature is Donkey Falls, Class 6. Take out on river right to portage. This drop has been run through the sneak route on extreme river right, but it is not recommended. After getting in below Donkey Falls, continue downstream until Bailey's Chute, taking out for the mandatory portage on river left. Hike the trail around Bailey's Chute and paddle downstream 1 more kilometre, taking out on river left. Hike up to the parking lot and your vehicle.

Camping: Camping is available at the provincial campsite just off Highway 5 at the town of Clearwater or in Wells Gray Provincial Park at Clearwater Lake Campground, the put-in location. Unorganized camping is available along River Road on the west side of the river at approximately kilometre 27.

Clearwater River – Middle

At a Glance: A very scenic run with challenging sections for more advanced paddlers. Sabre Tooth can get the heart beating a little faster! The run is generally beside the road and some of the more difficult sections can be scouted from the road.

Best Time of Year: late summer or early fall. Check the river gauge before starting your run. The gauge is found on the first cement bridge on the Old North Thompson Highway Road heading upstream (the bridge in town). The river gauge can be seen on the south upstream side of the bridge.

Maps: 92-P/9, 92-P/16. Kamloops Forest Region Recreation Map, Clearwater Forest District Recreation Map.

Also, stop at the visitor centre at the junction of Highway 5 and Clearwater Valley Road to check on a park permit, maps of the park, and road, weather and camping conditions in the park.

Contact the centre at:
Wells Gray Information Centre
Box 1988, RR1
Clearwater B.C. V0E 1N0
Tel: (250) 674-2646

Rating: Class 4

Length: 13km

Time: 2 to 6 hours depending on put-in

Shuttle time: 15 minutes

Hazards: find take-out or risk running the Kettle, a Class 6 rapid

Getting There: From Prince George, drive south on Highway 97 to Highway 24 East to Lone Butte and Little Fort. Follow Highway 24 to its end at Little Fort on Highway 5. Drive north on Highway 5 to the town of Clearwater, following the signs leading to Wells Gray Provincial Park.

Alternately, drive east on Highway 97 from Prince George and then south on Highway 5 to the town of Clearwater. Driving time and distances are very comparable to the directions given above.

Take-out – The Kettle: Just before entering Clearwater from the south, look for Old North Thompson Highway Road on your left.

Turn onto this road and follow it to the first cement bridge. Check the water levels on the gauge at this bridge. Continue up the Camp 2 Road for less than a kilometre, and turn right onto what the locals refer to as the River Road, an old forestry road.

As you drive up the road, look for The Kettle Rapid at kilometre 9; you should see a yellow steel gate. This is the 9km take-out. Get out and take a good look. There is a big pool of Class 1 water river-wide; make sure you take out on the river here as Class 6 Kettle Rapid is immediately downstream.

Put-in – Kilometre 22: Continue up the road further to kilometre 22 and put in here. Some of the river can be scouted during the drive.

Alternate Put-in – Kilometre 14: Continue up the road to kilometre 14 and put in here. Some of the river can be scouted during the drive.

Description: Below the put-in at kilometre 22 the river is Class 2 and there are a couple of good play spots to warm up in within the first km before Sabre Tooth. Sabre Tooth is a big, big, big wave that crashes like ocean surf. This can be scouted from the road near kilometre 20 before you are on the river. The Sabre Tooth drop is Class 4. After this drop is a long paddle on Class 2 water until approximately kilometre 13. Here there are more play waves in a Class 3 to 3+ canyon that continues for 3km leading down to the take-out. The take-out at kilometre 9 is marked by a large, river-wide, Class 1 stretch of water. Immediately below the take-out is the Kettle. This Class 6 rapid has been run a few times in low water but is definitely not recommended (unless you have a death wish!)

Beginners Park and Play Wave

There is a great park and play surf wave for beginners located at kilometre 28 when the scale reads 3, usually in July or August. Drive up the river road further to kilometre 28 and put in at the washboard gravel road. The Class 2 wave is big and glassy, an excellent spot to learn to surf!

Camping: Unorganized camping is available along River Road at approximately kilometre 27. Camping is also available at the provincial campsite just off Highway 5 at the town of Clearwater or in Wells Gray Provincial Park at Clearwater Lake Campground.

Paul Walsh

Pink Mountain is just one of the many great spots on this popular play river.

14 Clearwater River – Lower

At a Glance: The Clearwater is appropriately named. After high water in spring, you can see the volcanic boulders magnified along the river bottom. The river is large and swift, making for big, roomy play waves and eddies. The first half of this run is full of wonderful Class 2 to 4 play waves and holes until tapering off to near flat by the end.

Best Time of Year: anywhere from 0 to 6 on the gauge. The play is prime between 2.5 and 4.5 on the gauge. The gauge is found on the first cement bridge on the Old North Thompson Highway Road heading upstream (the bridge in town). The river gauge can be seen on the south (upstream) side of the bridge.

Maps: 92-P/9, 92-P/16, Kamloops Forest Region Recreation Map, Clearwater Forest District Recreation Map.

Rating: Class 4

Length: 9km

Time: 3 hours

Shuttle time: 15 minutes

Hazards:
- avoid Hole in the Wall
- avoid M-87 at high water

Also, stop at the visitor centre at the junction of Highway 5 and Clearwater Valley Road to check on a park permit, maps of the park, and road, weather and camping conditions in the park. Contact the centre at:

Wells Gray Information Centre
Box 1988, RR1
Clearwater B.C.   V0E 1N0
Tel: (250) 674-2646

Getting There: From Prince George, drive south on Highway 97, turn left onto Highway 24 East to Lone Butte and Little Fort. From Little Fort, drive north on Highway 5 to the town of Clearwater, following the signs leading to Wells Gray Provincial Park.

Alternately, drive east on Highway 97 from Prince George and then south on Highway 5 to the town of Clearwater. Driving time and distances are very comparable to the directions given above.

Take-out: Just before entering Clearwater from the south, look for Old North Thompson Highway Road on your left. Turn onto this road and follow it to the first cement bridge (this is the bridge in town). The take-out is 100m upstream of the bridge on the river right side. Check the water levels on the gauge at this bridge.

Put-in – The Kettle: To do the full Lower run, continue up the Camp 2 Road for less than a kilometre and turn right onto what the locals refer to as the River Road, an old forestry road. Put in at kilometre 8 below the Kettle (a Class 6 rapid); there is a moderate hike to the river.

Alternate Put-in – Three Fingers: Alternately, put in at the raft put-in located about 500m down the road from the first put-in just below the Three Fingers Drop.

Description: Before starting your descent, walk upstream along the trail to have a look at the Kettle. Late in the season you may see Chinook and Sockeye salmon making their way up the Kettle. Starting from the Three Fingers put-in just below the Kettle is the Three Fingers drop, Class 3+ to 4. Looking downstream from the Three Fingers drop, you can see a giant wave on the left called The Wall. To run the Three Fingers, a ledge-hole dropping into boily, pushy water, the most common routes are river left and river centre, past the raft put-in.

This leads you to The Wall in the left channel around an island. Note that the right channel has extremely difficult ledges and holes and is not recommended. The Wall is a large, glassy surf wave found at the top of the island. Unfortunately, this wave is a one-timer, so make sure you catch it on the way down as you won't get a second try. Below The Wall along the island, the river is a turbulent Class 4 rapid. Notwithstanding the large volume of this river, paddlers have reported hitting their heads on rocks at the bottom of this rapid. At the bottom of the island below The Wall, there is another great surf wave on river right with a small eddy. At certain water levels, there is a small pour over that forms behind the wave that you want to avoid as it can be quite sticky.

Below the island at the confluence of the two channels is M-87, a huge almost river-wide whirlpool, Class 3+ to 4. Run the river on the left side between M-87 and the re-circulating eddy. M-87 really starts working at higher water levels, around 6 on the gauge; at lower water levels it should not pose a problem.

Continue down river catching lots of one-time surf waves. There are approximately 6 rapids below M-87 with occasional large holes that can be easily avoided if you read the river well. At the Rock Wall, look up on the river right shore, searching for a hole/window rock formation. This is your clue that Tsunami is ahead of you about 500m. This is a river-wide surf wave that you can't miss even if you have to hike back up! Below Tsunami is Goose Rock. Eddy out on the left above Goose Rock. Hike up from here for another round at Tsunami.

Downstream, there is Buckaroo, a very big, fast, bouncy wave, as well as Pink Mountain. Pink Mountain is on the river left side and has good eddy access. This is a large wave with a nice foam pile, excellent for surfing and spinning moves. The last 3km down to the take-out are relatively uneventful. The take-out is on river right before the bridge.

Camping: Unorganized camping is available along River Road at approximately kilometre 27. Camping is also available at the provincial campsite just off Highway 5 at the town of Clearwater or in Wells Gray Provincial Park at Clearwater Lake Campground.

Cottonwood River

This medium sized river is generally swift flowing and has several very exciting Class 4+ canyons. Intermediate paddlers will be challenged on the two main drops in the Upper section while advanced paddlers will find the many drops contained in the Middle section exhilarating. Beginner paddlers can paddle the lower section if guided by an intermediate paddler. Different water levels can change this river dramatically, so be sure to check the river gauge.

Graham Gerry

Pinball is worth the wade back upstream when it's prime as shown here.

15 Cottonwood River – Upper

At a Glance: This is a medium volume river. It has three technical pool-drop rapids that can provide some heart stopping excitement and good training for advanced runs. The rapids on the Middle Cottonwood are similar in size, but much more continuous.

Rating: Class 3+ when under 2.2 on the gauge; Class 4+ when over 2.2 on the gauge. Less than 0.5 on the gauge is considered low and more than 1.8, high. The gauge is located at the take-out and is painted on one of the bridge pylons on river right.

Best Time of Year: The Cottonwood River is fed primarily by rain and local snowmelt. The local runoff creates high water early in the spring. This is the prime paddling season, usually lasting for one or two months. Continuous heavy rains will bring the water level back up later in the season. The best surfing can be found when the water level is between 1.0 and 2.1 on the gauge.

Rating: Class 3+ to 4+

Length: 6km

Time:1 to 4 hours depending on water levels and scouting

Shuttle time: 15 minutes

Hazards:
- log jams
- sweepers
- sticky holes

Maps: 93-G/1, Cariboo Forest Region Recreation Map (East)

Getting There: The Cottonwood River is located about 15km north of Quesnel. From Prince George, drive south on Highway 97 to the town of Hixon. From here continue south on Highway 97 for 41.5km to the bridge over the Cottonwood River.

Take-out: Just before getting to the Cottonwood River Bridge on Highway 97, turn into the "Area of Interest" pullout on the left. There is a spring at the north end of this pullout where you can fill up your water bottles. Take the road leading down to the river; this is the take-out. Check the water level gauge on the bridge pylon.

Put-in: Travel north from the take-out back along Highway 97 for 2.2km and turn right onto Umiti Pit Road. From here the roads form a bit of a maze, but the turns you need to take are marked with pink tiger-striped flagging. Drive east along this road and turn right onto the spur road at the 3km marker. Head southeast for approximately 700 metres then turn right. Turn left at the junction 1.4km further along. There is a sharp right corner another 1.2km along the road. The road becomes very steep past this point. If it is very wet, or if you don't have a 4WD, you should park here and carry your boats the last 3km to the river (you can take a short-cut down a gravel bank). Vehicles with good traction and good clearance can drive the remaining distance to the put-in. A deserted vehicle marks the spot. You'll have to carry your boat down a bank to get to the water.

Alternate Put-in: Access is also possible on river left, an 18km shuttle, by way of Highway 97 South. Follow Highway 97 south past the Cottonwood River Bridge 3.5km to McLean Road. Turn left on McLean Road and follow it until it ends at the Barkerville Highway. Turn left onto the Barkerville Highway and follow it 9.5km east to a wide, unmarked mining road. Turn left onto the mining road (16.7km from the junction of Highway 26 and Highway 97) and travel 5km to the river.

Description: The river starts out easy with a few small surfing waves. The best surf wave on the river is usually found 1.0km from the put-in. It is a steep wave in the middle of the channel, with a big eddy on river left. The river continues with a few small drops, one of which (Pinball) develops into an awesome river-wide surf wave at 1.9 on the gauge. Unfortunately, there is no eddy below Pinball at high water levels, and you have a tough waist-deep slog upstream to get a second chance at it.

A few hundred metres below Pinball (2km from the put-in), there is a sharp left corner in the river, and it becomes obvious that you are entering the first canyon. The canyon has continuous waves and a few holes for 250 metres and ends with a big Class 3 to 4 rapid called Kickoff. Kickoff should be scouted to ensure there are no log jams. When you see the horizon line, eddy-out on river right and scramble along the rocks. The rapid often makes intermediate paddlers' stomachs sink the first time they see it. Portaging is difficult and the large pool below the drop can seem like the only forgiving feature. At low water, the rapid is bony and fairly technical, requiring a boof and a sharp right turn to avoid a possible pin. Between 1.0 and 1.8 on the gauge, Kickoff is pushy and fairly chaotic. Above 1.8, most of Kickoff's features wash out. The easiest line is down middle right at all water levels.

Graham Gerry

Kickoff is the first of this section's large rapids

The flat water below Kickoff continues for approximately 5km. When you see the concrete retaining wall below the railway bridge, eddy-out on river left and walk along the trail to scout the last two rapids on the run, JimmyJackJoe and Volcanic Eruption. Below 2.0 on the gauge, a boulder splits the river in half at JimmyJackJoe, Class 2+ to 4+. This boulder forms a huge haystack at high water levels. The easiest line (except at very low water levels) is down the middle of the left channel. Below 0.3 on the gauge, the left channel contains a tight, horizontal hole that takes a few solid, well-timed paddle strokes to punch. At this level, river right is an easy, but bony, slide. The river right channel contains formidable hydraulics above 1.0 on the gauge, and is usually avoided by all but the most aggressive paddlers.

Below JimmyJackJoe, there is a short pool before you drop into Volcanic Eruption, Class 3 to 4+. At normal water levels, the easiest line down Volcanic Eruption is by starting in middle left and moving quickly to far right. Below 0.5 on the gauge, a fun 3-foot high waterfall forms on far left. Volcanic Eruption is named because of its appearance in full raging flood. It has never been run above 2.2 on the gauge. A huge wave train washes over the mid-stream boulder and smashes instantly into the volcanic haystacks below while frightening pour-overs form along the right riverbank.

Graham Gerry

Running Jimmy Jack Joe attracts an audience

15 Cottonwood River - Middle

At a Glance: This fast-paced river has plenty of adrenaline rushes for even expert paddlers. Great play holes and drops are cause for excitement on this narrow canyoned, scenic river.

Best time of Year: zero on the gauge, which is likely to occur in May or June. The gauge is under the Highway 97 Bridge over the Cottonwood River on the river right pillar.

Maps: 93-G/1, Cariboo Forest Region Recreation Map (East)

Getting There: Take Highway 97 south from Prince George to Hixon. Set your odometre to zero here. Drive 25.5km further on Highway 97 and turn right onto Olson Road (just before Ahbau Creek). If approaching from the south, Olson Road is 15km after the Cottonwood River Bridge on Highway 97.

Take-out: Drive for 8km on Olson Road and turn left at the T-junction indicating Quesnel/Hixon (the Old Cariboo Highway) and continue to the bridge over the Cottonwood River (11.5km from the T-junction). There is a good take-out downstream of the bridge.

Rating: Class 4+

Length: 5 to 6 km

Time: 3 hours

Shuttle time: 20 minutes

Hazards:
- constricted drops
- steep walled canyons
- log jams

Put-in: Return to Highway 97 and continue south for 16.5km to the Cottonwood River Bridge. Just before getting to the Highway 97 Bridge across the Cottonwood River, turn into the "Area of Interest" pullout on the left. There is a spring at the north end of this pullout where you can fill up your water bottles. Take the road leading down to the river; this is the put-in. Check the water level gauge on the bridge pylon.

To save time, instead of backtracking to Highway 97 from the take-out, you can get to the put-in by driving 9.5km further past the Cottonwood River on the Old Cariboo Highway and turning left onto Ten Mile Lake Road North. Take this road for 6km back to Highway 97, staying right at all junctions. At Highway 97, turn left driving north to the Cottonwood River Bridge.

Description: The river starts with approximately 3km of Class 2 to 3 rapids interspersed with flat water and then a Class 3 canyon that is about 800m long. After the canyon, the river continues with another 3km of flat water. The river then narrows again to a canyon to the first major drop, The Hallway. Scout this drop looking for potential river wide log jams.

There is then a short 200m section of Class 2 water before you should take out on river left to scout Tax Relief. Tax Relief is a short Class 4+ drop named so because there are only two things certain in life - death and taxes. If you make a mistake here, you won't have to pay taxes anymore! This rapid has several straight drops into a seething cauldron (The Receiver General). You can portage Tax Relief on river left – termed Tax Evasion - but you can't avoid the Receiver General!

Hardy Griesbauer

Dropping into Tax Relief

Graham Gerry

The paddler for whom the drop was named makes peace with "Honest Gamble" - 0.3 on the gauge

The river then does a dogleg to the right and then immediately to the left with Class 4 rapids interspersed with small pools. When you come to Honest Gamble (Class 4), there is a house- sized rock in the centre of the river and then two short 4 foot waterfalls about 50 feet apart. This is followed by a short 50m flat stretch before a straight Class 4+ slot called Take Me Home Sweet Jesus. This drop was run for the first time in 2000, but you will want to scout/portage on river right. There is a seal launch from the right bank and then a dogleg left which smashes into a head wall. Many interesting lines through this exist, but they all end up in The Daughters of Krishna, a 1km series of five significant ledge drops with holes (Class 4). There is a final drop approximately 2km from the last Daughters of Krishna called Surprise that is Class 4 and can be run on river left. Forty minutes of Class 1 and 2 water leads to the take-out on river right below the Olson Road Bridge.

Camping: Free camping is available at the take-out, but there are no facilities. There is a good campground with a sandy beach at Ten Mile Lake Provincial Park 5km south of the put-in on Highway 97.

15 Cottonwood River – Lower

At a Glance: A very good beginner kayak run or canoeing day trip close to Quesnel.

Best Time of Year: medium water levels from mid-May to mid-July

Maps: 93-G/2, 93-G/1, Cariboo Forest Region Recreation Map (East)

Getting There: Take Highway 97 south from Prince George to Hixon. Set your odometre to zero here. Drive 25.5km further on Highway 97 and turn right onto Olson Road (just before Ahbau Creek). If approaching from the south, Olson Road is 15km after the Cottonwood River Bridge on Highway 97.

Take-out: Drive for 8km on Olson Road and turn left at the T-junction indicating Quesnel/Hixon (the Old Cariboo Highway). The Cottonwood River runs adjacent to the Old Cariboo Highway just upstream of the Ahbau Creek Bridge approximately 1km from the T-junction. There is a pullout for vehicles on the left side of the road (an alternate access location).

Rating:Class 2

Length: 15km

Time:
1 hour for kayak run
7 hour canoe run to Quesnel

Shuttle time:
10 minutes for kayak run
45 minutes for canoe run

Hazards:
•log jams
•sweepers

Continue on the Old Cariboo Highway past the Ahbau Creek Bridge and turn right onto Tertiary Road. Take the last left off this road through a field to the river. A pipeline valve on the left side of the road marks this turn. If you go straight, you end up at a farmhouse. Walk to the river to mark the take-out location.

Alternate Take-out - Quesnel: A option suitable for canoes is to take out in Quesnel turning the trip into a full day trip. To do so, drive south on Highway 97 to Quesnel. Highway 97 turns into Front Street in downtown Quesnel and runs adjacent to the Fraser River. Continue straight on Front Street past Carson Avenue and look for an entrance to Ceal

Tingley Park, the first right after Carson Avenue. The park is located at the junction of the Fraser and Quesnel rivers. On the river, the take-out to the park will be on river left. Use caution when approaching the bridge pylons at Quesnel.

Put-in: Drive for 8km on Olson Road and turn left at the T-junction indicating Quesnel/Hixon (the Old Cariboo Highway). At the T-junction turn left and continue to the bridge over the Cottonwood River (11.5km from the T-junction). There is a good put-in downstream of the bridge.

To get to the put-in from Ceal Tingley Park in Quesnel, drive north on Highway 97. Turn left at the fifth set of lights from Ceal Tingley Park, Quesnel - Hixon Road. Stay on this road until you come to the old bridge crossing the Cottonwood River.

Description: This is one of the best runs in the Quesnel area for beginner kayakers and makes for a nice canoeing day trip. The run meanders a lot and there are many log jams that paddlers should be wary of. There are a few play waves along the way and plenty of eddies to practice turns in. Downstream of the second take-out, the river is braided and there are many log jams. Watch for floating debris on the Fraser River at higher water.

John Marien

Novice paddlers will enjoy a trip on this portion of the river.

Camping: Unorganized camping is available at the put-in, but there are no facilities. There is a good campground with a sandy beach at Ten Mile Lake Provincial Park 5km south of the Cottonwood River Bridge on Highway 97, or 20km south of Olson Road on Highway 97.

These falls on Herrick Creek were once considered for hydroelectric power generation. The canyon has not been paddled.

Paul Walsh

My Dog is Drowning

Four kayakers are learning to roll at the Nechako River boat launch. The group includes a trained instructor with two able assistants, a medical doctor, a naturopath, an industrial first aid graduate, a fitness instructor with first aid training, and an athletic swimmer. They have flashy dry suits and safety gear - they are ready for the river.

Meanwhile, about fifty feet away, a woman is walking her dog. Her husband tags along too. The dog decides to take a swim and ends up on a clean, distinct little eddy line at the boat launch. The dog is repeatedly drawn out into the main current, so hubby goes in for the rescue. He too starts recycling along the eddy line.

The woman freaks. "Help, help! My dog is drowning! So is my husband!"

In seconds, seven paddlers rush to her side. "Oh boyoboyoboy! We get to rescue a swimmer! We get to try our CPR!"

Just as they arrive, dog and hubby break free and swim to shore. "Darn! No rescue."

The woman turns to find herself surrounded by the S.W.A.T. wearing coloured suits, carrying throwbags, and sporting emergency knives. Her face flushes. She apologizes for all the trouble.

They apologize, "Sorry we took so long."

16 Crooked River

The Crooked allows you to get a jump on paddling season because it is the first river to open in the spring. Historically, the Crooked River was important as a transportation route connecting the Fraser River to the Peace River. Prospectors on their way to the gold fields of the Yukon used the Huble portage trail and the Crooked River on their journey north. Now the Hart Highway parallels the river quite closely, which results in traffic noises, but also an endless number of put-in take-out possibilities.

Several day trips are possible on the Crooked. The most obvious day trip for people starting from Prince George runs from Summit Lake to100 Road. The upper part of this run has some beaver dams.

Put-in #2 to the 100 Road is great in early spring because the whole length is navigable and provides the chance to get fairly close to trumpeter swans. The section from 100 Road to Davie Lake is highly recommended during the summer because it has lots of fun riffles, sand bars for swimming, and is possibly the best section for viewing wildlife. An interesting week-long trip could run from Summit Lake to McLeod Lake and then carry on to Williston Lake via the Pack River (see Pack River trip reports).

Rating: Class 1 to 2

Length: 95 km for entire river

Tiime: 4 to 5 days for entire river

Shuttle time: less than 30 minutes between adjacent put-ins

Hazards:
- sweepers
- narrow river bends
- fast water during spring run-off

At a Glance: The Crooked River system is comprised of a series of small lakes and pools joined by short river sections. These river sections are sometimes narrow, windy, and lined with sweepers, making manoeuvring tricky. The river is spring fed, so sections of it stay open all winter and provide ideal habitat for trumpeter swans and waterfowl. Bird and wildlife viewing is always excellent but especially so in early spring when the swans are still there. This exceptional area is only 40 minutes from Prince George.

Length and time for sections

	Length	Time
Summit L. to 100 Road:	15km	5 hours
100 Road to 200 Road:	17km	4 hours
200 Road to Davie Lake:	10km	3 hours
Davie Lake to Kerry Lake:	29km	7 hours
Kerry L. to McLeod L.:	24km	6 hours

Best Time of Year: late March to October, excluding spring run-off

Maps: 93-J/7, 93-J/10, 93-J/15, Prince George Forest District Recreation Map

Getting There: From Prince George, drive north on Highway 97 and turn left on Talus Road, 3.5km north of the Summit Lake turnoff.

Put-in - Summit Lake: Take the first right turn off Talus Road and drive to the bridge, crossing the Crooked River near the start of the Teapot Mountain hiking trail.

Access #1 - BCR pullout: On Highway 97, approximately 7.3km north of the Talus Road, there is a very small, short BCR pull out / access road on the left side of the highway where the road, railway, and river converge. When you are on the river, this point is easily recognized because it comes so close to the railway and road.

Access #2 - 100 Road: Drive 14.5km north of Talus Road on Highway 97 to The Pas Lumber 100 Road just before the level railway crossing on Highway 97. Turn left onto the 100 Road and drive 1.5km to the bridge crossing the river. A small turnoff leads to a parking area on the right just before the bridge.

Access #3 - 200 Road: Drive 1/2 km past the gas station at Bear Lake and turn left onto the Bear Lake/Davie 200 Road. A bridge crosses the river in approximately 4.5km.

Access #4 - Davie Lake: Drive 4.7km north of the service station at Bear Lake and turn left at the Davie Lake sign; go 1.6km to the Forest Service Recreation Site on the lake.

Access #5 - Redrocky Lake: Drive 17.7km north of the service station at Bear Lake, turn left onto a grassy strip then come back south about 200m to a gap in the willows on the shore of Redrocky Lake

Access #6 - Kerry Lake: Drive 22km north of the service station at Bear Lake, turn left and follow the access road 1.1km to the lake.

Take-out - McLeod Lake: Continue north from Bear Lake, and when you see McLeod Lake, watch for signs to the provincial park at Whiskers Point.

Description: Immediately downstream of Summit Lake, the river is lake like for about 1.5km. It then narrows and speeds up as it snakes along. Here, it is obvious how the river got its name. The narrow winding sections contain many willow sweepers and some beaver dams. Depending on water levels, you may have to drag your canoe over the dams. The sweepers can be dangerous in high water, espe-

James Taylor

Trumpeter Swans are one of the species that make this trip a favourite for birders.

cially in narrow sections of the river. Approximately 7km after Summit Lake, the river widens into deep pools and lakes. It continues like this to the 100 Road except for two faster, narrow, windy sections. The highway is never far away, often within earshot.

Between 100 Road and 200 Road, the river is deep and wide with almost no current for the first 6.5km. As it nears the boundary of Crooked River Provincial Park, it turns south-west, passes an old road bridge, then narrows and speeds up. There is a good campsite on the right bank shortly after the start of the narrow section. Overhanging willows and hairpin bends can create some difficulties so be prepared to wade occasionally. At times the stream divides and contains small log jams. Be prepared to carry over 3 or 4 beaver dams. Avoid this section in high water because the water floods a large area of impenetrable willow thicket and getting to dry land can be difficult if you capsize. The river regains a more defined channel about 6km below Dominion Creek and passes a canoe only access forest recreation site with excellent camping. The river has some gentle chutes through low, forested hills down to the 200 Road Bridge.

Just below the 200 Road Bridge, there is a shallow riffle, but after this the channel becomes deep and remains like this to Davie Lake. The current is slow but steady for 5km, and the river is wide enough to allow easy navigation. Sand bars in this section provide good lunch and swimming spots, and in lower water they provide good campsites. The river then begins to meander and progress seems very slow. At Davie Lake there are three Forest Service Recreation Sites on the right (east) shore.

Follow the east shore of Davie Lake to a wide marsh through a narrows with a silver cabin on the right. There is no obvious flow in the 2.5km of marsh but keep to the right in the open water, double back south-east for 300m just before the current appears. Angusmac Creek enters on river right about 200m later; there is a large gravel bar there except at high water levels. The channel is deep, slow, and windy all the way to Redrocky Lake. It could easily be run at higher water levels, but there would be no dry landing spots except where the river nears the highway, 3km before Kerry Lake.

For a short side trip, turn left into a long bay as soon as you enter Redrocky Lake and visit the ruins of a fur ranch circa 1940. Most of Redrocky Lake below the take-out is visible from the highway but Kerry Lake is more secluded and offers interesting lake paddling with several bays and two islands. Between Kerry Lake and McLeod Lake, the river is wide and the current fairly slow. Whiskers Point Provincial Park, on McLeod Lake is approximately 4km north on the east side.

Camping: Camping is available at several Forest Service Recreation sites along the river. The first of these is at Summit Lake near the put-in. The Crooked River Canyon Forest Service Site is located on the left two thirds of the way from the 100 bridge to the 200 bridge (there is no canyon!). There is also a site on river left just below the 100 Road Bridge, three sites on Davie Lake (all on the east side) and one site on the south-east end of Kerry Lake. Camping is also available at two provincial parks, one at Crooked River Provincial Park near Bear Lake, the other at Whiskers Point Provincial Park, which is the take-out. Unorganized camping is available along the river, but it is scarce and not recommended.

Alan Lamb

Lost on Davie Lake.

Crooked River Provincial Park (Bear Lake)

At a Glance: A very small lake for paddling, but the beach and Livingston Springs are the main attractants.

Length: 0.5km

Maps: 93-J/7, Prince George Forest District Recreation Map

Getting There: From Prince George drive north on Highway 97 past Summit Lake. Turn left into the park just south of the community of Bear Lake.

Description: This park has a very popular swimming beach and is often quite crowded on a sunny summer day. To circumnavigate the lake takes less than an hour, but it is a safe location for children to learn to paddle and for you to practice your self-rescue in the warm water.

Camping: The park provides treed sites that can be busy on a long weekend.

Wayne Giles

Moose are frequently sighted in spring.

18 Dahl Lake

At a Glance: Dahl Lake is a fairly short drive from Prince George, and because motor boats are not permitted, it is a great place to enjoy a quiet paddle. Moose, beaver, muskrat, and water birds are commonly seen.

Maps: 93-G/14, Prince George Forest District Recreation Map. Other information is available from BC Parks Prince George Office, Box 2045 (4051 18th Ave.), Prince George, BC, V2N 2J6. Telephone: (250) 565-6340.

Getting there: Starting at the junctions of Highways 16 and 97, drive west on Highway 16 for approximately 40km. Turn left at the sign "Berman Lake Regional Park" and drive past Berman Lake to Normal Lake. At kilometre 16, just before the cabins appear, look for a cart track on the left hand side of the road. Drive down this track for 100m to a parking lot.

Length: 3km

Time: 0.5 to 2 days

Best time: mid-May to mid-October

Description: Dahl Lake is connected to Norman Lake by a short narrow stream. The entrance to the stream is approximately 500m from the put-in, along the left-hand (south) shore. There are numerous islands on the lake and an irregular shoreline, which makes interesting paddling. Trees grow right to the edge of the lake, so the islands are the best stopping places.

Camping: There is a picnic spot and possible campsites at the put-in on Norman Lake. Dahl Lake itself has no official campsites, but numerous islands have been cleared to allow small campsites. As well, what appears to be an old sawmill site in a large cove on the east side of the lake provides camp spots.

Doré River
(3.3km on South Fork to Highway 16 Bridge)

At a Glance: More of a creeking style of run, this run has continuous whitewater requiring good river reading skills to miss the many large holes. Rolling might not be pleasant with the shallow water and many rocks to avoid. Some portions are constricted. The mountain scenery of the McBride area is spectacular if you have a chance to look up while speeding along. The river drains out of the valley between Belle Mountain and Lucille Mountain, two popular recreation areas in McBride.

Rating: Class 4

Length: 13km

Time: 2 hours

Shuttle time: 15 minutes

Hazards:
- log jams
- fast shallow water
- keepers

Best Time of Year: Spring during medium to high water.

Maps: 93-H/1, 93-H/8, Robson Valley Forest District Recreation Map

Getting There: From Prince George drive on Highway 16 east to the town of McBride. Approximately 4km before McBride you will cross the Doré River.

Take-out: At the Doré River Bridge on Highway 16. Take out on river right upstream of the bridge.

Put-in: Drive up the Doré River Forest Service Road for approximately 12km along the west side of the river to a junction in the road. Much of the river is visible on the drive up. Take the left fork (South Doré Forest Service Road leading to the Eagle Valley trailhead) and cross the Doré River (an alternate put-in). The right fork leads up the West Doré River Forest Service Road to the Ozalenka trailhead. Continue up the South Doré Forest Service Road for approximately 3.3km and pull out where you can most easily scramble down to the river.

Description: The upper portion down to the confluence of the south fork and west fork of the Doré River (or first bridge when paddling down stream) is continuous white water with few eddies and many rocks and holes to avoid (class 3 to 4-). Punch through holes and try to clear your vision before you hit the next one. The river moves quickly throughout allowing little time for reading the water so grab good eddies when you can to re-group. Downstream to the highway the river is class 3+ throughout with a few class 4 slightly more constricted areas. The first of these areas is approximately 1km downstream of the confluence. The river narrows and is divided by a large rock in the center. This rock can be seen from the road at a distance on the trip in. Stop and have a look to check the channels are clean. The second one is just downstream of the second bridge when paddling downstream (or first bridge when driving up the road). Much of the run can be scouted from the road though many of the bigger rapids are not visible. Don't be fooled, get out of the car and have a look. Swimming would be ugly so have a good safety plan.

There are several locations where logs could easily block the entire river and create a significant hazard. Log jams in several locations are also dangerous as staying upright near them is not guaranteed.

The last two kilometers down to the highway bridge is the easiest portion, class 2+. There is very little canyon along the entire run and the road is almost always within easy reach if portaging is necessary.

Camping: Beaver Falls on the Holmes River. To get there, travel east on Highway 16 to McBride. The highway crosses the Holmes River about 11km east of the town of McBride. Just east of the Holmes River Bridge, turn left on the Holmes Forest Service Road and drive approximately 2km to a popular forest service site above Beaver Falls.

Eskers Provincial Park

At a Glance: Eskers park includes gently rolling hills (eskers) and many small lakes that support a wide variety of esker wetland birds and mammals. One canoeing option is to launch at Circle Lake, easily accessible from the first parking lot. A more strenuous option is to put-in on Camp Lake, 2.3km from the main parking lot, and paddle through a chain of small lakes to Kathie Lake. This unique wilderness canoe retreat is just 40km from Prince George.

Maps: 93-J/2, Prince George Forest District Recreation Map. A park map is usually available at the park's information booth, or from BC Parks Prince George Office, Box 2045 (4051 18th Ave.), Prince George, BC, V2N 2J6. Telephone: (250) 565-6340

Getting there: Drive north from Prince George, either on the Hart Highway or Foothills Boulevard, and turn left onto Chief Lake Road. The park is approximately 40km west. Signs to the park are poor although signs in the park are good.

The put-in to Circle Lake is 200m from the first parking lot on a wide, well maintained trail. To put in at Camp Lake, drive past Circle Lake. Look for the service road sign and gate 100 metres before the main parking lot. To save steps, drop your canoe and gear here and park in the lot. The service road is also identified on park maps as the "snowshoe route." The trail is flat, easy and ideal for a wheeled canoe walker. There are two canoe rests beside the trail.

Length:
Circle Lake 2km
other lakes 0.5 to 3km

Time:
Circle Lake 1 to 2 hours
lake chain half a day

Hazards: none

Best time: May to November

Description: Circle Lake - This tranquil lake is wheelchair accessible and has a large floating dock. An enclosed building offers shelter from the elements. The lake has five marshy areas on its shoreline, which makes it perfect for watching birds, aquatic creatures and larger animals. The beaver makes its presence known with dens and cuttings, and moose paths crisscross the marshes. The sounds of nature are seldom disturbed.

Camp Lake to Kathie Lake - You may wonder whether the effort of portaging in this park is worthwhile. It is! The first portage, at the end of Camp Lake, is approximately 800m and spans an esker. The remaining portages are an easy 30 to 50m. At the head of each portage is a floating dock. These docks make it easy to land and also provide good markers for the beginning of each portage.

The large number of eskers make for fascinating paddling. Eskers are hilly ridges of sand and gravel deposited in the melting water of retreating glaciers. These landforms continue underwater where they rise eerily in the clear water to greet the paddler, then drop away. Some eskers rise out of the water to form small islands, which dot the larger lakes. These islands are an excellent place to stop, rest, and eat. Animal trails are evident on the surrounding hills and beaver trails dot the shoreline.

Camp and Kathie Lakes are less than 3km in length and 1km in width. The remaining three lakes are less than 1km. Their size, combined with the eskers, creates an intimate mood and virtually eliminates wind and waves. There are trout in all lakes, and fishing is good in Camp, Kathie and Bow Lakes. You may be rewarded with a school of rainbow or brook trout swimming under your canoe anywhere. The real joy of these lakes is the solitude and crystal clear water. Visibility in the lakes exceeds 10 metres.

Camping: There is no camping in the park.

Marian Tamkin

A group of paddlers prepare to do an after work run on the Nechako River into town.

Paul Walsh

It's hard not to spend the entire time relaxing on one of the sandy beaches of these regional parks; Clearwater Lake in Wells Gray Provincial Park (top) and West Lake Provincial Park (bottom).

Fergus McNab

21 ferguson lake

Ferguson Lake

At a Glance: This is a very handy, small lake located within Prince George city limits, and is ideal for getting a little practice in on canoe strokes or a quick paddle. Many varieties of birds and ducks can be seen on the lake.

Maps: city street map, 93-G/15

Getting There: Drive north on the Hart Highway (Highway 97) to Kelly Road North (found on the left shortly after Chief Lake Road). Drive for approximately 1km on Kelly Road North and turn left at Ferguson Lake Road. Follow this road for 1km on paved surface and then continue straight on gravel road for 2.8km to Ferguson Lake Park on the left.

Length: 0.5km

Time: 1 hour

Hazards: none

Best time: May to November

Carry your canoe down to the water a short distance from the parking lot and launch at the dock.

Description: This is a small lake, several hundred metres across and not even a kilometre long. It has marshy shorelines and therefore plenty of bird life. Motorized boats are not permitted on the lake, so enjoy the quiet as you explore the shoreline.

Camping: none

Fergus McNab

The many lakes in the region are a great place to take children

Wayne Giles

There are many trips left to explore in North-Central BC that aren't in this book including the Gataga River pictured here.

Fraser River: Mount Robson Provincial Park to Quesnel

The Fraser is ranked with the world's great rivers. It runs for 1375 kilometres from its headwaters in the Rockies to the Pacific Ocean flowing through an amazing number of environments along the way. It supports a rich diversity of animal and plant life, as well as human settlements, farms and industry. Although the lower Fraser is populated and polluted, the upper region (described in three separate reports in this book) remains fairly wild, although there are some farms and a few communities. The water is mostly Class 1 except for three short canyons, and one long white water section that contains Class 3 to 5 rapids. This whitewater section runs from Red Pass to Mount Robson campground and is a popular day trip for advanced white water paddlers. This run is described in a separate report.

Heather Myers

The Rocky Mountains in the Robson Valley.

Mount Robson Bridge to Red Pass

At a Glance: This is the most upstream section of the Fraser you can reach by road. The river is small and the water clear as it flows through beautiful snow-capped mountain scenery.

Best time of year: mid-summer to fall when water levels are low to medium. Refer to water flow graph on the following page.

Maps: 83-D/15, 83-E/3, Robson Valley Forest District Recreation Map

Getting there: From Mount Robson Provincial Park on Highway 16 east of Prince George.

Take-out - Red Pass: Drive east on Highway 16 from Mount Robson up a steep hill to Red Pass. Just west of Moose Lake, there is a railway "Y" turnaround on the south side of the highway. You will see the rail line come to an end, perpendicular to the highway. Do not plan to paddle further downstream because the water becomes very dangerous and is only suitable for expert paddlers in closed boats (see Fraser River – Upper trip description).

Put-in: Drive east of Mount Robson Provincial Park campsite and Moose Lake to a bridge crossing the Fraser River just west of Lucerne Lake.

Description: Below the put-in, the river contains cold glacial water and flows quickly through spectacular mountain scenery. The water is Class 2 to 2+ for approximately 16km and then becomes Class 1 to Moose Lake. The take-out is at the west end of this picturesque lake, at Red Pass station. There is plenty of wildlife to spot, including moose, deer, black bear, coyotes and wolves. Fishing is excellent and very large Dolly Varden and Lake Trout have been caught in Moose Lake.

Rating Class 1 to 2

Length: 37km

Time: 2 easy days

Shuttle time: 0.5 hours

Hazards:
•cold water
•sweepers

Camping: Camping is possible at the east end of Moose Lake; most other camping opportunities would be on gravel bars during lower water. Check at the Mount Robson Information Centre to find out about camping regulations.

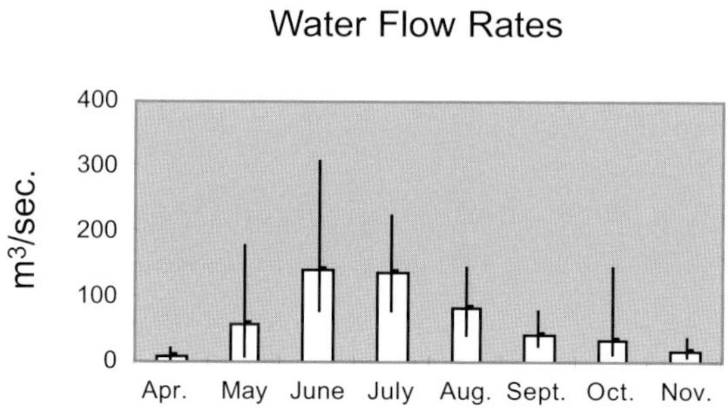

Ian Norn

Not a place for the timid, this boater practices some advanced moves on the Upper section.

Fraser River - Upper: Red Pass to Mount Robson

At a Glance: This is a world class run for the advanced paddler. This exciting stretch of the river is situated in the spectacular scenery of Mount Robson Provincial Park. Expect plenty of tough drops and great play in the cold, clear water.

Best Time of Year: May to July is high water - serious adventure seekers (expert paddlers). August to October is low water - advanced paddlers. Refer to the water flow graph on the preceeding page.

Getting There: Travel east past McBride on Highway 16 to Mount Robson Information Centre. Reset your odometre here.

Put-in Section 1 – Railway Y: About 14km East of Mount Robson Information Centre on Highway 16 and 2km past the pipeline road of Section 2, a road will be on the right toward the end of a straight stretch. This road goes steeply down the bank from the highway but can be driven by a 4WD. Stay right on the road until you arrive at the main line. Carry across the tracks and you will be at the put-in.

Rating: Class 4+
Class 5 waterfall

Put-in Section 2 – Pipeline Road: About 12km east of Mount Robson Information Centre on Highway 16, a side road with a steel gate will be on the right. Carry about 300m down to the river.

Time:
Section 1 - 1 hour
Section 2 - 2 to 3 hours
Section 3 - 1 hour

Put-in Section 3 – Overlander Falls: Watch for the tourist signs to Overlander Falls and take the trail down to the falls.

Hazards:
- complex rapids
- monster holes
- steepboulder gardens
- sweepers
- log jams
- Overlander Falls
- extremely cold water

Take-out: Turn right off of Highway 16 directly across from the Mount Robson Information Centre. Continue on this road approximately 2km past the campground to a bridge across the Fraser River. Just across the bridge there is a small road leading down to the river, this is the take-out for the full run.

Description: Each of the three sections described below could be run as separate trips or combined for one great whitewater day trip.

Section 1: From the start it is an easy float and warm up for the good things to come. The steepest drop in this section is just below the railway bridge. Eddy out on river left above the bridge. From here the river continues downhill at a good clip creating nonstop waves all the way to the first take-out. An island will appear on the right as the main flow of the river drops sharply to the left. This is about 5km on the river from the put-in. Take the right channel and take out at the bottom of the island. Work your way up to the pipeline road. This is a nice clean run with a great wave on the right just above the island you are looking for to end the first section.

Section 2: About 1km below the islands, the river heads toward the railway tracks and a structure that looks like an outhouse appears on the left. Shithouse Rapid is just beyond. This rapid should be scouted on river left. Eddy out on the left, right below the first big wave to scout the rest of the rapid, which includes a river-wide hole. This section, from the wave to the hole, is generally run left of centre following the main flow. Just around the corner from the hole, after a straight stretch, is Eric's Hole, which takes up most of the river width. The best route around it is to go right down a shallow, rocky channel. At the bottom you may see an attractive rooster tail wave. There is a large sharp rock in the middle of it, so avoid it. From here down to the Toilet Bowl there is quite a bit of Class 3 with three Class 4 sections. A good rule to follow here is to go with the main flow.

When you hit a calm section, you know you are near the Toilet Bowl. A set of cliffs will appear on the right. Eddy out on the left to take a look. Once around the corner, the river continues to drop steeply with many flushy holes. Soon the highway appears high above you on the right. The third time you come back to the highway brings you to Staircase. This is best scouted from the highway. At the bottom of Staircase stay right and take out on the corner.
Section 3: Just below Staircase there are a number of great play spots. Caution - Soon you will see some mist rising and you will be

at Overlander Falls. Take out on the right if you do not want to run the falls. The canyon section follows. If in doubt, go left. When things open up again, you will come to a river-wide ledge pour over. The easiest route is in the middle. Below here it mellows for a short bit, then the canyon starts to narrow and the speed picks up. Several large holes appear in succession and the speed increases. When the canyon gets very narrow again and the river is tending to the left again, you know you are very close to the Terminator. This can be an ugly drop! It is best to scout this one before you decide whether or not you want to run this section, as it is a horrendous hike up to the trail. Below Terminator it is an exhilarating run to the bottom of a large eddy with a road right down to the river, the take-out for Section 3.

Camping: Organized camping is available at Mount Robson Provincial Park near the take-out.

Ian Norn

The canyon just below Overlander Falls.

22 Fraser River - Tete Jaune to Quesnel

fraser river

At a Glance: From Tete Jaune, the Fraser flows northwest through the Rocky Mountain Trench bordered by Rocky Mountains to the north and Cariboo Mountains to the south. The trench is actually a wide valley, which becomes wider as it progresses northwest. Near Prince George, the river leaves the mountains, turns south and flows through the Interior Plateau to Quesnel. Although the Fraser is mostly Class 1, it quickly becomes a very large river with strong hydraulics. Canoeists interested in paddling this whole section should anticipate three possible portages where the river courses through narrow canyons that produce Class 2+ to Class 4 water.

Length and time of sections:

Tete Jaune to McBride:	100km	2 days
McBride to Penny	140km	3 days
Penny to Limestone Creek:	110km	4 days
Limestone Cr to Pr. George	90km	2 days
Prince George to Quesnel	150km	3 days

Rating: Class 1 to 2
canyons Class 2+ to 4

Length: 590km

Time: 2 weeks

Shuttle time:
•total trip - 5 hours
•between adjacent points - 2 to 3 hours

Hazards:
•logpiles between Tete Jaune and McBride
•boils and strong eddy lines below McBride
•narrow canyons with strong hydraulics

Maps:
Tete Jaune to McBride 83-D/14, 83-D/13, 83-E/4, 93-H/1, 93-H/8
McBride to Penny 93-H/8, 93-H/7, 93-H/10, 93-H/11, 93-H/14
Penny to Prince George 93-H/14, 93-H/13, 93-I/4, 93-J/1, 93-J/2, 93-G/15
Prince George to Quesnel 93-G/15, 93-G/10, 93-G/7, 93-G/2, 93-B/15, 93-B/16
Robson Valley Forest District Forest District Recreation Map, Prince George Forest District Recreation Map

Best time of year: mid-summer to fall when water levels are low to medium. Flow rates taken at Shelley.

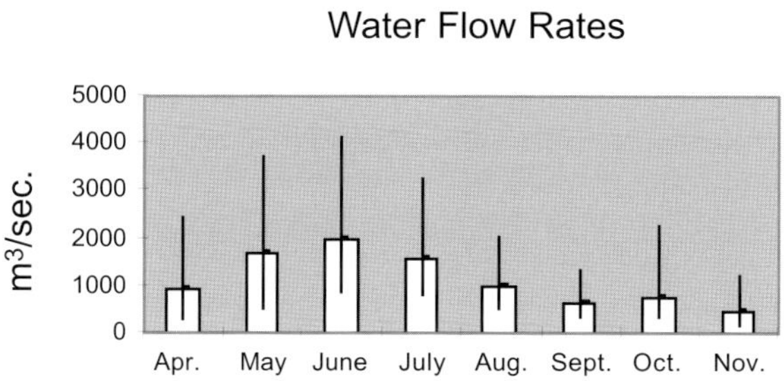

Getting there: All access locations with the exception of Limestone Creek are off Highway 16 east. In addition to those listed below, you can also access the Fraser at Dunster, Crescent Spur, Dome Creek and Longworth. Access #4 must be accessed from Highway 97 north.

Put in - Tete Jaune: At Tete Jaune Cache, just west of the junction with Highway 5, turn off Highway 16 into the motel/gas station. Multi-day parking is usually permitted at the back of this property.

Access #1 - McBride: At McBride, where the highway bridge crosses the river. Ask for permission to park vehicles at local restaurants or motels just up the highway. You can also park at the waste transfer site by the bridge.

Access #2 - Penny: Turn left from Highway 16 onto the Penny Access Road, approximately 100km from Prince George. Drive a few kilometres to a parking lot across the river from Penny.

Access #3 - Limestone Creek: Drive north on Highway 97 and turn right onto the North Fraser Forest Road (2km past the turnoff to Huble Farm). Drive 37km along the North Fraser Road. Between kilometre 37 and Limestone Creek Bridge, there is an open area with a gravel bank leading to the river.

Access #4 - McGregor: Turn left onto Upper Fraser Road 18km east of Prince George. Drive approximately 60km to the Hansard Bridge over the Fraser near the old town site of McGregor.

Access #5- Prince George: Cottonwood Island Park on River Road in Prince George is at the confluence of the Nechako and Fraser Rivers.

Take-out - Quesnel: Drive south on Highway 97 to Quesnel. Highway 97 turns into Front Street downtown in Quesnel and runs adjacent to the Fraser River. Continue straight on Front Street past Carson Avenue and look for an entrance to Ceal Tingley Park, the first right past Carson Avenue. The park is located at the junction of the Fraser and Quesnel rivers.

Description: From Tete Jaune to McBride, the valley is fairly wide and the Fraser winds through farmland bounded by the Cariboo Mountains to the south and the Rocky Mountains to the north. Oxbows and meanders offer alternating views of these ranges. The farms, framed by mountains, create a charming ambiance. Cows are frequently spotted, but so are deer, coyotes and black bear; the latter are especially common during salmon spawning in late summer. The river contains many gravel bars and shallow areas after mid-summer, and it may be necessary to get out and pull your canoe. After the entry of several creeks and the Raush River, the volume increases, resulting in some Class 1+ waves at the corners. Log jams are common but easy to avoid in low to moderate water levels. The shoreline in many places is not very accessible because of logs and steep mud banks (about 4-6' high). This valley is known for its westerly winds.

Below McBride, there is less development although small settlements do exist at the historical railway stops of Crescent Spur, Dome Creek, and Penny. These communities are tiny and do not have services. The river continues to meander through the wide mountain valley and, at lower water levels, many sand bars are exposed. The only rapids between McBride and Penny are the Goat River rapids located a few kilometres below the confluence of the Goat and Fraser rivers. Rated as Class 2, these rapids are easy to avoid and in some water levels are not noticeable. Many people choose to take out at Penny in order to avoid the Grand Canyon, approximately 40km downstream. Proceed past Penny only if you are prepared for two strenuous portages on rough trails that allow you to bypass the canyon.

The Grand Canyon includes two sections separated by a wide, slow stretch. These sections are created by water surging through narrow passages of volcanic rock, and each is rated from Class 2+ to 4 depending on water levels. At lower water, with careful reconnaissance, the canyon might be run; however, at high water it should be portaged.

Mike Nash

The first section of the Grand Canyon.

Historically, a variety of boats, rafts, and stern-wheelers navigated through here carrying passengers and freight between Yellowhead Pass and Fort George. Although most trips were successful, many people capsized and lost their lives. The famous Greens Rock, responsible for many of these deaths, has since been blasted. However, the tranquil appearing water can still be dangerous. The late Ray Mueller of Sinclair Mills, who worked the river from 1925, reported that on one of his trips through, without warning, a large tree catapulted out of the water and narrowly missed his boat both on exit and re-entry.

The canyon begins shortly after Kenneth Creek and is marked by a rocky outcrop on river left. Pull in on the beach just upstream of this outcrop to scout the top of the first section. This section runs straight for approximately 800m then takes a sharp right turn where it runs the same distance again. Between these two straight sections is a huge eddy on river left where it would be possible to regroup and bail if necessary. Run both sections on river left to avoid the large standing waves and some squirrely sections on river right. The entire canyon can be portaged on a trail on river left or short sections can be portaged on river right. After a slow section the second canyon begins. In medium water levels this section contains no hazards.

Downstream of the Grand Canyon, the river is Class 1 and becomes relatively slow. It leaves the mountains near Sinclair Mills and flows through evergreen and broadleaf forests of the Interior Plateau. A short distance after Averil Creek, the river reaches its most northern point, called North Bend. From here the Fraser turns south and passes the historic Huble Farm. It is well worth stopping here to witness the enactment of life as it was over 100 years ago. Huble Farm was also the start of the twelve kilometre portage from the Fraser, over the Arctic-Pacific Divide, to Summit Lake. Approximately 3km downstream of Huble Farm, the Class 2 Giscome Rapids run for about 2km. These rapids consist of large standing waves and rocks. The river is very wide here and there is no preferred route. After the rapids, the river is an easy float to Prince George. Several kilometres before Prince George, the river flows through an industrial section where pulp mills dump effluent into the river, degrading the quality of the already muddy water.

Downstream of Prince George, the river continues to flow through attractive evergreen and broadleaf forests. The same species of wildlife common on the upstream stretches can be spotted here. The entire stretch is Class 1 except for Fort George Canyon (also known as Red Rock Canyon), and Cottonwood Canyon. Fort George Canyon is locat-

Heather Myers

The river near McBride offers huge mountain scenery.

ed 26km downstream of Prince George and is marked by a large island midstream. A few breakers on river left are the only warning that the canyon is approaching. The river divides into many channels between rock islands and makes a slight left turn. In low water the entire rapid can be run on river left. In higher water levels a dangerous whirlpool develops on the left side of the third small island, so it is best to run to the right of this island. Scouting and portaging is possible but difficult because of the high banks and dense bush. If problems occur, a hiking trail at the beginning of the canyon on river right leads to West Lake Road.

The river becomes Class 1 for the next 90km. On this stretch, the community of Stone Creek provides basic services. An interesting historic landmark is located a few kilometres upstream of the confluence of the Blackwater River. A sign high on the banks marks the beginning of the famous West Road (Blackwater trail) that Alexander Mackenzie took on his historic journey to the Pacific Ocean. Cottonwood Canyon is approximately 5km above the confluence of the Cottonwood River. The canyon is marked by an island on the left just before the river bends slightly to the right. In the canyon, the river narrows considerably and the velocity increases; there are large standing waves with strong eddy lines on both sides - Class 2. At high water these waves approach 2m, pushing the Class to 3. Run through the centre. The river mellows to Class 1 past the confluence of the Cottonwood and Fraser rivers and continues this way to Quesnel.

Camping: Sandbars and sandy shorelines provide camping during low water, but camping would be problematic in high water. There are some good possibilities on banks downstream of McBride. Organized campsites are located at Forest Service Recreation sites at the confluence of McLennan River near Tete Jaune, and at the junction of Averil Creek, just upstream of North Bend.

Grand Canyon of the Fraser[2]

In the summer of 1862, several groups of fortune seekers travelled overland from Canada to Barkerville. They crossed the prairies with Red River carts, but forest travel became arduous by the time they reached Tete Jaune Cache. There, they built rafts and canoes and floated down the Fraser. Here is an extract from a trip report by one of their leaders, Thomas McMicking published in the New Westminster British Columbian.

On Tuesday afternoon, when, according to our reckoning, we had made 70 miles from the Cache, we came upon a portion of the river which flows through an exceedingly level country; and where the sluggish stream, widening out the distance of fully a mile, does not run at a faster rate than two miles an hour. The mountains here recede to a considerable distance from the river, and at times disappear altogether, leaving a wide valley of nicely timbered land, with here and there an occasional opening. The soil appeared to consist principally of an alluvial deposit, which had accumulated during the successive ages of time, from the debris of the mountains above.

The character of the river and of the country through which it flows continued much the same during the following two days, Wednesday and Thursday, the 3rd and 4th September, interrupted only by two or three slight rapids. Our progress here was so slow that, in order to accelerate our motion, we had side oars rigged upon our raft, by means of which we doubled our speed. We also passed through, on the 4th, what the Indians had attempted to describe to us as a lake, but which was nothing more than a considerable expansion of the river. On Friday the country became more broken, and the current of the river much swifter. Hitherto our progress had been uninterrupted by any misfortune; we had been sailing steadily onward for five days, and were just beginning to entertain feelings of security, and to congratulate ourselves upon our good fortune in having escaped the dangers we dreaded. But at half-past 5 o'clock in the morning of Saturday, the 6th, we were suddenly startled by an unusual roaring noise that broke the stillness of the morning, the cause and source of which was soon explained by the lookout shouting, "Breakers ahead!"

2 Thomas McMicking, published in New Westminister British Columbian, approximately 1862

We had reached the big rapids, and we were already so near them and were being swept toward them by the current so rapidly that we had barely time to row ashore and make fast before we were drawn into them. After landing we went some distance along the shore to examine the place before we should attempt to run it. We found that the rapids consisted of three distinct stretches, with small bays or eddies of comparatively quiet water between, which had evidently been formed, at some remote period of time, by the stream breaking through as many parallel ridges. The banks on both sides are very rocky and precipitous, and the channel, which is very narrow, and obstructed in many places by pointed rocks, contained six sharp angles through which the pent-up and maddened waters rushed with violent and resistless impetuosity. It seemed like presumption to think of risking our lives through such a perilous place; but we saw no alternative, we had either to run the rapids or starve where we were. We found a passage by which we could make a portage around the first two stretches, but were unable to get over the rocky bluffs of the third.

At length Mr. Harkness decided to try it, if we would lighten the raft by a number of us making the portage, leaving only men enough aboard to man the oars. About ten men remained on the raft, and the balance of us stationed ourselves along the shore where we might possibly be able to render some assistance if it were required. Everything being ready the ropes were untied and the frail bark pushed into the current. Onward they swept like an arrow. They seemed to be rushing into the very jaws of death. Before them on the right rose a rocky reef, against which the furious flood was lashing itself into foam, threatening instant and unavoidable destruction, and on the other side a seething and eddying whirlpool was ready to engulf in its greedy vortex any mortal who might venture within its reach. With fearful velocity they were hurried along directly towards the fatal rock. Their ruin seemed inevitable. It was a moment of painful suspense. Not a word was spoken except the necessary orders of the pilot, which were distinctly heard on shore, above the din and tumult of the scene. Now was the critical moment. Everyone bent manfully to his oar. The raft shot closely past the rock, tearing away the stern row-lock, and glided safely down into the eddy below. The agony was over. The gauntlet had been run, and all survived. The issue of the ordeal was announced by an involuntary cheer from the brave hearts aboard the raft, which was heartily responded to by those on shore.

The last part of the rapids was less dangerous than what we had already passed and we ran through it in safety, all hands being aboard. The scene we have described was re-enacted as each raft arrived at the canyon, and notwithstanding the imminent dangers that surrounded them, all succeeded in escaping them. Less fortunate, however, were those who attempted to run the rapids in canoes; and here the saddest part of my narrative begins.

A canoe, carrying three of the Toronto party, Messrs. Carroll, McKenzie, and Patterson, was the first to leave Tete Jaune Cache, and, as it ran considerably faster than the rafts, it arrived at the rapids two days before the first raft. Those who first reached the place after them were surprised to find this party still there. Their canoe, which contained their provisions, tent, clothing, blankets, and even their coats, had foundered while they were attempting to let it down the canyon by means of a lariat, and everything belonging to them was swept away by the current. During the interval that elapsed between this occurrence and the arrival of the raft they were exposed to all the inclemency of the weather, which at the time happened to be very cold and rainy, without food, clothing, or shelter. Mr. Patterson, one of the party, had been complaining before he left the Cache, of some slight affection of the throat, which was greatly aggravated by exposure. This canoe was followed by two others, fastened together, carrying Messrs. Robertson, Warren, and Douglas, of the Goderich party, who shared even a worse fate than those who preceded them. They had only reached the first ripple when their canoes were suddenly caught by one of the whirls and capsized, throwing them and all their goods into the river. Mr. Robertson, being a good swimmer, immediately quitted the canoes and struck out for the shore, at the same time advising the others, who could not swim, to cling to them. This they found to be a very difficult matter, as the canoes were kept continually rolling over and over in the rapids. They however succeeded in maintaining their hold and as they came to the surface at each revolution of the canoes, they could see Mr. Robertson still manfully contending with the angry waves, while at each opportunity he would encourage them to hold fast, apparently more concerned for their safety than about his own welfare. At length the canoes drifted upon a shoal by which they were enabled to make a small island in the middle of the stream. After regaining their feet their first thought was to look after their companion. But he was nowhere to be seen. He had sunk to rise no more in this life.

The remaining two threatened to be even worse, as they had no means of escaping from the island upon which they had been cast; and but for the timely arrival of the rafts of the Huntingdon party, who rescued them from their perilous situation, they must have perished also. I would fain wish that my record of fatal disasters might end here; but the chapter of accidents at this unfortunate spot is not yet concluded. Of the parties that succeeded us, two, namely: Mr. Carpenter, of Toronto, and Mr. P. Leader, of the county of Huron, Canada, were drowned by the upsetting of canoes under similar circumstances.

Immediately after passing these rapids the channel again widens out and the current becomes quite sluggish. The country, too, assumes something of the same aspect as that above the canyon.

Mike Nash

The ledge at the start to the first section of the Grand Canyon.

23 Goat River – Milk River to Highway 16

At a Glance: This river offers scenery, history, play opportunities and challenge. The river carves deep in the grandeur of the snow-capped Cariboo Mountains just west of McBride and tumbles into the Fraser River. You can easily see a short section running along Highway 16 for about 100m before crossing the highway. This delightful gem escaped notice for many years and, until recently, had only been paddled a few times. The historic Goat River Trail, a pack trail used as early as 1886 to connect McBride to Barkerville, follows much of the run.

Best Time of Year: medium water, lower water levels could be bony

Maps: 93-H/7, 93-H/10, Robson Valley Forest District Recreation Map

Getting There: Drive 165km west of Prince George on Highway 16 to the bridge crossing the Goat River.

Take-out: At the picnic site at the Highway 16 Bridge over the Goat River.

Rating: Class 3
Class 4 to 5 canyon

Length: 16km

Time: 3 hours

Shuttle time: 25 minutes

Hazards:
•log jams
•narrow canyon

Put-in: From the Highway 16 bridge over the Goat River, drive 4km east on the highway to the top of a hill (35km west of the town of McBride). Look for a good gravel road heading south (past the Goat River East Pit Road turn-off); turn right and drive approximately 13km where you will reach another road that turns right and goes downhill to the mouth of the Milk River. At the bridge just upstream of the confluence of the Milk and Goat rivers is a trail that leads down to the river. During the shuttle, the canyon can be scouted at kilometre six, but it is a tough hike down from the road.

Description: Many years ago, the now deceased Dane Wray first explored this river, and since there was no road access, he was forced to drag his kayak through miles of bush to reach the put-in. Even now, the access road is high above the river, and escape from the main canyon involves an ugly climb through devil's club. Because the river is small and runs quickly from snow-capped peaks into a tight canyon, water levels vary considerably and can dramatically change the character of the river, especially at the narrowest part of the canyon.

This Class 3 to 5 river is excellent water for those with adequate skill, equipment and organization to overcome its hazards. This trip should only be run with good leadership and well-chosen water levels. It is particularly important to know where to take out and scout (and possibly portage) the canyon.

Roy Howard

A small volume river running swiftly out of the North Cariboo Mountains.

The trip starts about 16km upstream from the highway, just above where the Milk River (appropriately named for its colour) enters the Goat. As soon as you put in, you realize how fast the Goat is as you speed downstream on easy roller coaster waves. You can spend all day playing on this run and never reach the highway. A few dangerous log jams decorate the ends of islands. Enjoy the magnificent views of Mount Sir Alexander and its neighbouring peaks on the trip down river.

The river can be divided into three sections: the upper, the canyon, and the lower. The upper portion consists of fast flowing water with many corners. The whole area is layered shale, thus creating many ledge drops on the outside bends; a deep eddy follows most drops.

About 500m past the second island is the start of the canyon. The river suddenly narrows and plunges through the first of two narrow chutes about

4 to 5 metres wide. Scouting is mandatory! The canyon can be scouted in either of two ways. During the shuttle, scramble down the steep creek ravine (located at km 6 on the logging road) to the canyon. Alternatively, the canyon can be scouted on the run by pulling out on river right.

The canyon consists of four rapids. The first one is the Slot, a narrow chute that becomes extremely dangerous at medium to high flows. The entire river drops about 1.5 metres into a large river-wide hole with a powerful backwash from which one might never emerge. Scout or portage on river right. Approximately 75m downstream from the Slot is the next rapid in the canyon, a short open area of rocky ledges and hydraulics that can be run to the centre of river left. This leads immediately into the third rapid, the Guzzler. Again, scout or portage on river right. The Guzzler is the second narrow chute with a violent hole on the left as you enter. This is followed by a headwall on river left that creates a large pillow twisting to the right. The ledge on the right can be run at most levels. Fortunately, there is a big pool immediately below this that gives you time to roll up before continuing down the canyon. The last rapid in the canyon, Bob and Ed's Boulder Dash, contains the biggest hydraulics in the river. It starts 100m downstream of the Guzzler. Scouting is recommended from river left. This section is straight with several huge boulders, big diagonal waves, and a big eddy at the bottom on river right. To avoid the ugly holes on the left, run right of centre.

Roy Howard

The clear water of the Goat attracts paddlers used to muddy rivers.

The first 3 parts of the canyon could not be scouted during a high water trip on June 7, 1990. The entire group dragged their boats up through the devil's club on the right bank to the top of a cliff, then lowered themselves on ropes before plunging into the last section. At lower water levels, it is possible to portage along the right riverbank and put-in using a glorious seal-launch off a smooth rock into the deep pool just past the Guzzler.

The lower section of the river below the canyon to the highway bridge, a half-hour paddle, is littered with gentle haystacks, small reversals, and prime surfing opportunities. At lower levels, this final part might be very bony.

NOTE: The Goat River above the Milk River junction to where the Goat River Trail leaves the river and continues into Bowron Park looks very kayakable, especially in high water, but access is restricted to a very long portage or helicopter. It has never been paddled.

Camping: There is a very good site on the Goat River Forest Service Road. Turn right at km 6 and follow the old road back to the cut block. There is a landing, perfect for camping as you come into the block. It even has an outhouse. The campsite is named Kopas Camp, after Cliff and Ruth Kopas (see story below), and it is signed thus on the logging road. This site is in the new West Twin Provincial Park. LaSalle Lakes Forest Service Site, approximately 5km west of the highway bridge over the Goat River also provides good camping.

Doug Radies

Winter is also a great time to visit the Goat River valley.

The Goat River Trail

The Goat River Trail was first roughly surveyed and cut out between Bowron Lake and the Fraser River in 1886 by men working for John Bowron, Gold Commissioner for the Cariboo. It is suspected by the Lheidli T'enneh to have also been a First Nations trade route prior to that, but hard evidence is lacking so far. It was then used extensively for moving goods and supplies back and forth between McBride and Barkerville and for prospecting along the lower reaches. The completion of the Grand Trunk Railway through the Robson Valley, in about 1913, saw a decline in use by packers. However, prospectors, trappers, hunters and adventurers continued to use the trail until the present day, although to a lesser extent in recent years, due to the lack of maintenance.

In 1933 Cliff and Ruth Kopas, from Okotoks, Alberta took their honeymoon by riding on horseback from their home in Okotoks to Bella Coola, BC. They rode the Goat River Trail as a significant part of their journey. A chapter on the trip through the Goat can be found in the book that Cliff later wrote about their journey, Packhorses to the Pacific. It is an excellent read, though currently out of print. A prospector/trapper/forest service cabin that was present when they made their ride, and may have actually housed them at the time, is still visible at the edge of the new West Twin Park at 6.5km on the Goat River FSR. There is ancient graffiti in this cabin from 1939.

Because of the heavy growth caused by an overabundance of moisture in the valley, there has always been an issue of maintaining the trail-- it's a big job, especially removing deadfall. The BC Forest Service maintained the trail from the 1920s or 30s until the mid-1970s, and then quit. Fraser Headwaters Alliance took over that role in 1998, and had the trail opened and clearly marked (a frequent complaint of trail users was the inability to find the trail), between the Milk River confluence and the logging road system just north of the Bowron Lake chain, by fall 1999.

The trail is gaining in popularity for its wilderness and heritage features. It has been selected, by the Federation of Mountain Clubs of BC, as a primary link in the National Trail - a foot trail planned to completely cross Canada. One group of nine hikers walked through the 50km between the Milk River and Littlefield Creek trailheads in September 2000; some actually hiked the 120km between the Fraser and Barkerville, as part of a trail dedication ceremony.

Holmes River (Beaver River)

At a Glance: While paddling through the boulder-strewn channels of this fast flowing mountain river, don't forget to look up at the beautiful vistas of the surrounding Rocky Mountains. The river has a fairly consistent drop throughout the run and has plenty of opportunity for play boating.

Best Time of Year: It is best run during spring runoff, typically from late May to early July.

Maps: 93-H/8, 83-E/5, Robson Valley Forest District Recreation Map

Getting There: From Prince George, travel east on Highway 16 to McBride. The highway crosses the Holmes River about 11km past the town of McBride. Just past the Holmes River Bridge, turn left on the Holmes Forest Service road that runs adjacent to the river (216km from Prince George).

Take-out: The Forest Service Site several kilometres up the road from the highway is the most common take-out location. There are many other opportunities to take out earlier on the river as the river frequently runs beside the road.

Put-in: Continue up the road 15km to where the road crosses the Holmes River. The put-in is on the downstream river- right side of the bridge.

Rating:
•Class 3+
•Class 4+ waterfall

Length: 13km

Time: 4 hours

Shuttle time: 20 minutes

Hazards:
•cold water
•log jams
•sweepers
•waterfall

Alternate Access: The Holmes Forest Service Road goes up the Holmes River about 60km into the heart of the Rockies (and nearly to Jasper National Park), providing river access at several points. Nearly the entire upper river, above the 15km bridge, is slow enough to be comfortable in an open canoe. There is plenty of water; the main obstacles are frequent log jams.

Description: This river is a true mountain river with beautiful scenery and fast moving, cold, clear water. At the put-in, you can try your luck at seal launching off the bridge, but it can be a bit of a 'gamble.' Foot pegs and heels have been known to be broken when the water level was too low! Downstream of the put-in bridge, the river starts off as Class 2 to 2+.

There are five major rapids and one ledge drop (avoidable on the left) along the course of the run. Each is a 3+ rating and can be river-scouted as you run them. These rapids vary in length from 400m to 1km. The beauty of them is that they are continuous action from the start. Swimming in any of these rapids is not a pleasant experience. Unless the swimmer is a proficient self-rescuer, expect to end up at the bottom of the rapid because the gradient, speed and depth of the water make assisted rescue difficult. Therefore, having a reliable combat roll in shal-

Wayne Giles

An exciting way to start the trip though ankles have been broken.

low fast water is a prerequisite for this run to ensure a good time for all.

Countless play spots punctuate the trip. Naturally, it takes a few trips on the river to scope them all out. High water levels tend to flush them out, but medium and even low water levels can be extremely playful. The local boaters count this as one of the premiere whitewater play runs. An added treat in the late summer is spawning Chinook salmon. The Holmes is one of the major spawning rivers in the upper Fraser, with some 2,000-3,000 spawners in August.

Camping: The Forest Service Site at the take-out offers very nice camping beside the river and a short walking trail to Beaver Falls.

Hardy Griesbauer

Running Beaver Falls is optional as it is located after the usual takeout.

25

horsefly river

Horsefly River – The Steps to Recreation Site

At a Glance: This is the most commonly paddled river in the Williams Lake area as it is close to town and can be paddled in the evening. This section of the river is quite scenic, and there is some good intermediate play boating on the holes and waves.

Best Time of Year: high water levels for The Steps section as many good play waves form. Medium to low water levels are recommended for the section from Rocky Bar to Forest Recreation Site.

Maps: 93-A/6, Cariboo Forest Region Recreation Map (East)

Getting There: From Prince George, drive south on Highway 97 to Williams Lake. Proceed 14km past Williams Lake and turn left onto Horsefly Road. Follow Horsefly Road east for 50km to the town of Horsefly.

Rating:
•The Steps - Class 3
•Rocky Bar to Rec Site - 2+

Length: 7km

Time: 2.5 hours

Shuttle time: 15 minutes

Hazards:
•log jams

Put-in – The Steps: In Horsefly, turn left on Boswell St. and drive to the fork in the road. Take the right branch, Quesnel Lake Road, to the end of the pavement. Drive approximately 6km further looking for a small gravel pit on the left side of the road. Park here. There is a fence line across from the gravel pit with a well-marked trail leading to the river. It's a 10 minute carry to the river.

Alternate Put-in – Rocky Bar: Drive a further 2.5km to the put-in at Rocky Bar. This is the first location that the road runs adjacent to the river after Horsefly. Put in here if you want to avoid The Steps rapid (see description below).

Take-out: Continue down Quesnel Lake Road a further 4km from Rocky Bar to a Forest Fecreation Site on the right side of the road.

Description: From the put-in for The Steps section of the river, it is a 20 minute float on Class 1 water to reach The Steps. The Steps is a river-wide ledge that drops about 8 feet on a big chute. The easier line is far river right. The left and middle can be run as well, but you are more in the maw of the drop. At the bottom of The Steps is a monster wave. Boaters must paddle hard to punch through this wave in higher water levels. The Steps would be very difficult to portage around.

Immediately below The Steps are two islands. It can be very swirly water here, so watch carefully for log jam hazards. Run either between the islands or to river left as the river right channel is jammed with logs. Below the island on the right is a fantastic surf wave with a great feeder eddy. The wave can be big, steep and fast if you catch it at the right water level. Continue down on Class 2 water to Rocky Bar.

Most of the river from Rocky Bar to the take-out at the Forest Recreation Site is Class 1 to 2 with numerous rocks to manoeuvre around. About 2km from the Rock Bar put-in, the river bends to the left and then funnels into a Class 2+ chute that piles into a headwall. Scout this rapid from river right at the top of the bend. Approximately 4km from the put-in, there is a Class 2 rapid with large standing waves and a boulder midstream. Below this rapid, the river bends to the left and funnels into a short Class 2+ chute with deep, calm pools below it. This chute is a fun lunch spot providing some excellent surfing opportunities. The river below this mellows to Class 1 until the take-out, approximately 1km later on river left.

Camping: At the take-out at the Forest Recreation Site.

McGregor River – Herrick Creek to Fraser River

At a Glance: This is a very pleasant wilderness trip that takes either 1 or 2 days depending on what section you choose to paddle. In the fall, soak up the rich colours of the trees and the views of the McGregor Range before entering the lower canyon, the scenic highlight of the trip and a good overnight resting stop.

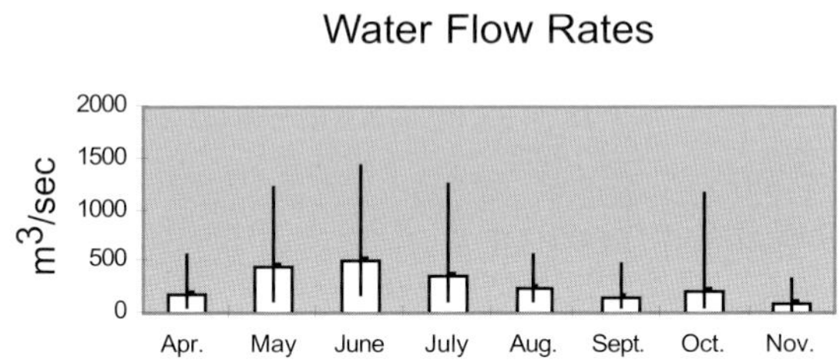

Best Time of Year: mid-June to fall. Flow rates taken at lower canyon.

Maps: 93-I/4, 93-I/5, 93-I/6, 93-J/1, Prince George Forest District Recreation Map.

Getting There: Starting at the Yellowhead Bridge in Prince George, drive east on Highway 16 for 14.5km and turn left onto the Upper Fraser Road. Follow this road past the town of Upper Fraser and cross the Fraser River on the Hansard Railway Bridge. This drive takes approximately 1 hour.

Rating: Class 1 to 3

Length: 73km

Time: total trip - 2 days

Shuttle time:1 hour

Hazards:
- riverboats
- log jams
- impassable canyon above Herrick Creek junction (can't portage)

Take-out – Church Road: You will likely want to arrange your shuttle by travelling to the take-out first. Immediately after crossing the Hansard Railway Bridge, turn left onto Church Road (North Fraser Road). Follow it for 18.5km to a bridge over the McGregor River. The best take-out is just upstream of the bridge on river left.

Alternate Take-out – Fraser River: Another possible take-out is located on the Fraser River, 11km down from the mouth of the McGregor, where the road runs adjacent to the Fraser River near Olson Creek. To reach it, take the left fork, the North Fraser Road, after crossing the bridge on the Church Road over the McGregor and proceed for 18km. If you use this take-out at the end of your trip, it is approximately 35km further along the road to Highway 97. This will take you to a point 16km north of the Salmon River Bridge.

Put-in: To reach the put-in on Herrick Creek, return via Church Road to Pass Lake Road at the old McGregor Camp. Continue up the Pass Lake Road for 45km (you will go by Pass Lake on your right) to the suspension bridge across the McGregor River above its impassable upper canyon. Immediately after the bridge, take the next left fork (Logan Road) and continue for approximately 21km until Herrick Creek becomes visible on your left. There is a good pull- out on the left immediately before Herrick Creek.

Description: From Herrick Creek to where the McGregor River joins, a distance of approximately 3km, the water is Class 1. The McGregor River enters on the left and is moderately fast Class 1 water before the lower canyon. Enjoy the mountain views in the upper part of the river. An aerial cable across the river signals that you have 2km to go to the head of the canyon. Just below the cable is a water monitoring station on river left which offers an escape route to the nearby road. There are a couple of Class 2 to 3 spots in the canyon, one near the start and one near the end, which can be sneaked by at lower water levels, but some turbulent spots near the vertical walls require care. This canyon is 6 to 7km long with steep rock walls at the entrance and lower end but some wooded slopes in the middle. Watch for an old trapper's cabin on river left just below the end of the canyon.

High-water

At higher levels, the river is swift Class 1+ above the lower canyon. The majority of the lower canyon presents little difficulty other than moderate turbulence, but scouting is difficult due to steep canyon walls, rocky cliffs, and heavy timber. No easy portage route exists. However, there are points where escape to logging sites is possible.

The entrance is Class 3 with waves from 1 to 1.5m high formed by a pressure ridge from river right. Some manoeuvring is required to avoid strong boils and hydraulics. A relatively calm and long, flat stretch below the first drop provides a chance to do rescues if necessary.

At the end of the canyon, vertical rock walls close in and the river makes a series of sharp bends. The final S-bend is Class 3 with no chance to scout. For the first right-hand sweep of the S-bend, run centre. Approach the left sweep left of centre. Be prepared for opposing cross currents, high standing waves, violent boils, and hydraulics. Avoid large drops behind rocky outcrops on either side of the canyon exit. Below the canyon down to the Fraser River, the river is swift moving Class 1. Watch for debris and log jams on the shore and islands throughout.

Note: Water levels on this river can fluctuate quickly. A group of local paddlers headed out to the river in mid-September expecting low water. However, recent rains in the watershed had swollen the river, and it raised an additional metre overnight as they camped near the put-in. The level that day was 4.0m at the McGregor gauge. This is only slightly lower than average levels for June, but still well below the peak of 5.7m set in 1990.

Camping: Unorganized along the river. At mid to lower water levels, there is a nice spot half-way through the canyon. There are forest service sites near the put-in and take-outs.

Wayne Giles

The lengthy canyon is the highlight of this trip.

Morice River

At a Glance: This river trip is renowned for its spectacular scenery around Morice Lake, clear waters, and excellent fishing.

Best Time of Year: July to September is generally the best time to run the river. For the best fishing, paddle in early October.

Maps: 93-L/2, 93-L/3, 93-L/7, Morice Forest District Recreation Map, Bulkley Forest District Recreation Map, Lakes Forest District Recreation Map,

Getting There: From Prince George, drive west on Highway 16 to the town of Houston. Approximately 2km past Houston, turn left at the sign indicating Northwood's (Canfor's) Houston Logging Operations.

Take-out: To take out at the island, drive down the Northwood Road (Morice Forest Service Road) for 27km to the first fork continuing up the Morice River. Take the right fork and after a further 3km, you will notice a bridge crossing the river onto an island that has been logged. The take-out is by the bridge.

Alternate Take-out: To complete the full trip and take out at the bridge, drive 4km on the Northwood Road (Morice Forest Service Road) and turn right onto another logging road that heads downhill to the Morice River. The take-out is across the bridge on the right side of the road.

Put-in: To reach the put-in at Morice Lake, proceed for 27km on the Northwood Road until you reach a fork in the road. Take the right fork. After another 18km, you will arrive at a second fork, just past Lamprey Creek. Take the left fork and drive 37km past Collins Lake and McBride Lake to Morice Lake. Put in

Rating: Class 1 to 2+

Length:
total trip - 83km
Morice Lake to Island - 49km
Island to Bridge - 34km

Time:
total trip - 3 days
Morice Lake to Island - 1.5 days
Island to Bridge - 1 day

Shuttle time: 1.5 hours

Hazards:
dangerous log jams

on the shore of Morice Lake. There are numerous roads turning off, but it is fairly obvious which is the main road to the lake.

Description: The scenery around Morice Lake is truly spectacular, and if time permits, it is worthwhile paddling up the lake to Atna Lake. Be careful to stay close to shore and have a day to spare as the wind on the lake can be quite dangerous to paddlers. If the wind is blowing the wrong way, you can be marooned until it dies down.

The Morice River is 2km northeast from the put-in. It is a medium volume river that is quite fast flowing. The colour is a beautiful blue-green, and it is crystal clear. The first section to Thautil River is Class 1-2 with a few boulders to manoeuvre around. It is mostly clear of log jams. The best campsite is at the junction of the two rivers; good spots after this are few and far between.

Once past Thautil River, the river splits into numerous channels that are full of log jams. This section requires paddling skills to avoid log jams, and because of its winding nature, a map would certainly be helpful. If you decide to paddle beyond the bridge crossing the river to the island, you should find a camping spot as near to the bridge as possible. The Morice canyon, Class 2+, is a few kilometres downstream and is best run after a good rest from paddling through the channels and log jams.

The canyon is preceded by a large S-bend in the river that is near the main road from Houston. At the end of the S-bend, eddy out on the left and scout the canyon before running it. The Class 2+ canyon is fairly clean with one log jam on river left and large standing waves in the centre.

Once past the canyon, the river mellows to Class 1 as it winds its way to Houston. The next bridge that crosses the river is the second take-out point.

Note: This river trip is renowned for its spectacular scenery around Morice Lake and its excellent fishing. A two day trip from Morice Lake to the first logging bridge past the Thautil River junction will give you a taste of both of these. To paddle further on to Houston is not really worth it due to the fire damage of the forests and the subsequent logging. The canyon is fun to run but not worth the extra day of paddling you will have to do to reach the next take-out.

Camping: There is a Forest Recreation Site with camping at the put-in on the shore of Morice Lake. Consider camping the first night out on the river at the junction of the Thautil and Morice rivers, a 4-hour paddle from Morice Lake. Unorganized camping is available at either of the two take-out locations.

James Taylor

The Willow River Paddlefest. The biggest paddling event of the year in Prince George.

Morkill River (km 48 to Cushing Creek at km 37)

At a Glance: This trip is a pleasant, non-threatening, Class 3 run that would be an excellent introduction to technical paddling for intermediate boaters. The scenery in the Morkill valley is worth the trip on its own, particularly if you can find all four known waterfalls. The 30m Morkill Falls, just below the bridge approximately 3km downstream from the take-out, are absolutely spectacular.

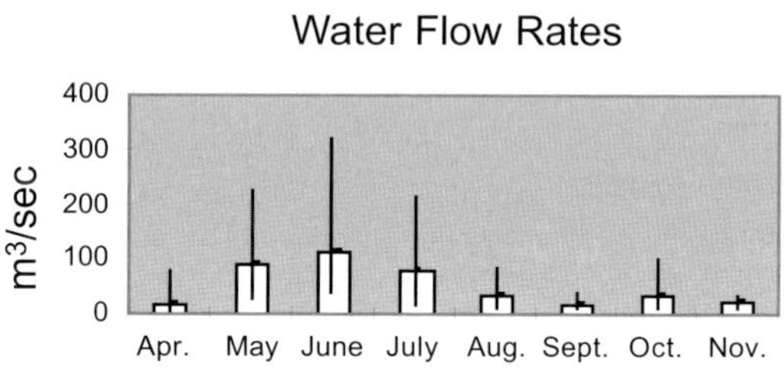

Best Time of Year: early summer, June or July. Flow rates taken below Hellroaring Creek.

Maps: 93-H/10, Prince George Forest District Recreation Map, Robson Valley Forest District Recreation Map

Rating: Class 3

Length: 10km

Time: 3 to 4 hours

Shuttle time: 15 minutes

Hazards:
- waterfalls to portage
- remote
- few eddies at high water
- sweepers

Getting There: From Prince George, travel east on Highway 16 about 165km to the turnoff on the left to the town of Crescent Spur. Follow this road north for 9 to 10km and turn right onto the Morkill Forest Service Road.

Take-out: Continue on the Morkill Forest Service Road, cross the Fraser River, and proceed up the Morkill valley to Cushing Creek at kilometre 37 on the Morkill Road. Just before the bridge over Cushing Creek, a road on the left leads 150m to a landing beside the river. This is the take-out.

Put-in: Proceed further up the Morkill road to kilometre 47.5 and take the fork to the right. Proceed another 150m and park. Carry 30 metres through the bush to the river.

Description: This run starts off with an easy Class 2 section for the first kilometre, followed by a Class 3 boulder garden. Approximately 1km into the boulder garden, there is a 4m stepped waterfall, "The Ankle Breaker", which almost all paddlers will want to portage. Take out on river right to scout and carry. These falls are also scoutable from the road at kilometre 46 on your way to the put-in. Following the falls is a steeper Class 3 boulder garden, which ends at approximately km 45.5 and is visible from the road.

After a 2km section of Class 2, a second Class 3 boulder garden starts. Halfway through this 1km section, the river approaches the road at kilometre 42.5. After another 400-500 m, the river drops through a tight "S" shaped gap. The approach to this spot is obvious – take out on river left to scout. The drop is runnable, but a partially submerged rock just below where the river piles into a large boulder on the right may cause problems.

Hardy Griesbauer

Enjoying the clear waters and tight boulder gardens.

Just after this drop is another 1km section of Class 2, followed by interspersed sections of Class 2 and Class 3 boulder gardens. All of the drops have clearly visible lines.

Warning: The take-out at Cushing Creek is mandatory! Just below the take-out is a 6 to7m waterfall. By itself, the waterfall may be runnable, but it is followed immediately by an extremely gnarly river-wide hole with only the slightest chance of a sneak route. Downstream of this hole, there is a 1km canyon that drops steeply, possibly ending in another waterfall (this section has not been explored).

Camping: There are Forest Service campsites located at LaSalle Lake (approximately 3km southwest of the Crescent Spur turnoff on Highway 16) and on the lower Goat River. Unorganized camping in the Morkill valley is also possible; a good potential site is located at the take-out.

Morkill Muddle - An Attempted First Descent

He came from New York to plant trees. He brought his kayak. He couldn't find anybody to paddle with, so he went out alone on the Morkill River. It was the first week of June and the river was running high and fast. The eddies were nearly non-existent and the water tumbled downhill rapidly.

He said he was an experienced kayaker, and he had a throw rope, but nobody to throw to. He didn't want to lose his gear if he swam, so he tied his rope from his kayak to the shoulder strap on his PFD.

He swam. His kayak plummeted downstream, dragging him head first. He fought to swing his body around to the `feet downstream' position. He jammed his feet down into a hole between the rocks. He found footing for a split second before the weight of the kayak pulled his upper body forward. His foot stayed in the hole, wedged between the rocks. His head went down, held under water by the rope and the kayak. He struggled helplessly to pull his trapped foot free. No such luck. He pulled on the rope. It remained taught. He realized he was going to die.

Suddenly the shoulder strap on his PFD ripped, and for a split second the rope went slack. The pressure on his foot eased, and he was free. He escaped, but the river ate his paddle, his PFD and his helmet. He says that next time he will tie the rope lower down, near his waist, so the force of the river won't pull him over.

Murray River

The Murray River is a medium volume river with clear water. The river's headwaters are in Monkman Provincial Park. The river then passes through the town of Tumbler Ridge, and flows down to meet the Pine River at Highway 97. The first section of the river, Kinuseo Falls to Tumbler Ridge, offers day tripping opportunities (jet boats use this upper portion for fishing) while the second section, Tumbler Ridge to East Pine, provides a very remote, spectacular multi-day canoe trip.

James Taylor

Beautiful scenery abounds on this trip through the Peace River Country.

29 Murray River - Kinuseo Falls to Tumbler Ridge

At a Glance: This is an attractive, medium volume, clear river that flows out of the beautiful mountains of the Monkman Range. Kinuseo Falls at the start of the trip are breath taking. Fishing along the upper stretches of the river is very good and draws many locals to the area.

Maps: 93-I/14, 93-P/3, Dawson Creek Forest District Recreation Map

Getting There: From Prince George, drive north to Tumbler Ridge.

Take-out: Highway 29 crosses the Murray River a short distance before Tumbler Ridge. A boat launch is located on river left downstream of the bridge. Flatbed Creek Campground is 1km further along the highway.

Put-in: Continue down the highway to Tumbler Ridge. From here, follow the signs along Highway 29 to Kinuseo Falls in Monkman Provincial Park. The road from the Quintette Mine to the falls is well-maintained gravel. You can drop your boat in the water at any of the bridges you cross along the gravel road into the park, the last one being at the 41.5km marker, or continue on to the falls. At the falls there is a well-maintained 1.5km hiking trail, which leads to the river. The trail climbs for the first 200m to a viewpoint of the falls and then drops 60m to a pool on the river just below the falls.

Rating: Class 2

Length: 51km

Time:
- total trip - 2 days
- falls to first bridge - 3 hours
- first bridge to mine site - 4 hours
- mine site to Tumbler R. - 3 hours

Shuttle time: total trip - 45 minutes

Hazards:
- log jams
- river boats

Description: The river is a clear, cold, medium volume river flowing out of the Monkman Ranges through the Rocky Mountain Foothills. The scenery on the first day is quite spectacular including views of the 60m Kinuseo Falls and the surrounding mountains of Monkman Park. The river is mostly Class 1 with a few easy Class 2 stretches and generally flows at a consistent rate. Residents of Tumbler Ridge use jet boats and jet-skis to travel up the river to view the falls and try their luck at fishing; however, powerboat traffic is not excessive. The river passes through the Quintette Mine site.

Camping: Organized camping is available in Monkman Provincial Park near the put-in at Kinuseo Falls. Along the river, camping is unorganized. A nice, treed campsite is located on the second island just downstream from the spectacular falls. You can line back upstream from here to view the falls. Further downstream, camping is on gravel/sand bars. The occasional hunt camp offers treed camping on the higher banks. Depending on timing, it is recommended that on the first night you select a campsite between the first and second bridge encountered when paddling down the river as traveling further will place you in close proximity to the mine site. Organized camping is available at Flatbed Creek Provincial Park on Highway 29 near the take-out.

James Taylor

Feeling dwarfed by the cliffs and cut banks throughout the trip.

Murray River - Tumbler Ridge to East Pine

At a Glance: This medium volume river flows through the Rocky Mountain Foothills on its way north, carving delightful canyons, some with steep walled cut-banks over 1000 feet high. Scenery is reminiscent of that in the Chilcotin Region. Ledges in the river provide for some excitement.

Maps: 93-P/2, 93-P/6, 93-P/7, 93-P/11, Dawson Creek Forest District Recreation Map

Getting There: From Prince George, drive north to Chetwynd and follow Highway 29 towards Tumbler Ridge.

Put-in: Highway 29 crosses the Murray River a short distance before Tumbler Ridge. A boat launch is located on river left downstream of the bridge; this is the put-in. Flatbed Creek Campground is 1km further along the highway.

Rating: Class 2 to 3

Length: 110km

Time: 2 to 3 days

Shuttle time: 2 hours

Hazards:
- log jams
- nearly river wide ledges

Take-out: Travel 25km east of Chetwynd on Highway 97 to the town of East Pine and access Pine River from the East Pine Provincial Park. To reach the take-out at the end of your paddle down the Murray, you will have to paddle a short distance up the Pine River to the take-out from the junction of the Pine and Murray Rivers.

Description: The river is generally Class 2 with some fun rollers and haystacks, but contains four, almost river-wide, ledges that must be avoided. This increases the overall river rating to Class 3. All the ledges are difficult to see on approach and must be scouted. However, all were runnable in low water after scouting. Runability is unknown at higher water levels.

The second and third ledges are marked on the topographic maps as rapids. The first ledge is 12km upstream of the two marked ledges. Pull out well ahead of the rapid and scout on river right and then on river left if necessary. A large, flat rock outcrop on river right is located approximately 1km before the two successive ledges marked on the topographic maps and provides a good warning that the ledges are just ahead. Scout on the left making sure you examine both ledges. The last ledge, which is river wide, is 8 to 9km upstream of the confluence of the Pine River. Scout this ledge on river left.

Camping: Organized camping is available at Flatbed Creek Provincial Park on Highway 29 near the put-in. Note that there is no camping at East Pine Provincial Park on Highway 97 at the take-out. On the river, camping is unorganized on gravel bars. The occasional hunt camp on the banks offers sites in the trees. Good sites can be scarce at times. However, numerous opportunities do exist 6 to 8km downstream of the marked ledges on the topographic maps along a very scenic stretch of the river.

James Taylor

Scouting one of the river wide ledges.

Murtle Lake

At a Glance: This canoe access only lake located in Wells Gray Provincial Park has it all! Enjoy fantastic sandy beaches, beautiful mountain hikes, and incredible fishing.

Best Time of Year: June to October

Maps: 83-D/4, Kamloops Forest Region Recreation Map, Clearwater Forest District Recreation Map.

For Clearwater/Blue River area information contact:

> Wells Gray Information Centre
> Box 1988, RR1
> Clearwater. B.C. V0E 1N0
> Tel: (250) 674-2646

Camping Reservations can be made by calling:
Discover Camping Campground Reservation Service
1-800-689-9025, www.discovercamping.ca

Length:
100km shoreline
north arm 25km
west arm 15km

Time: 2 to 7 days

Hazards:
high winds/waves

At the time of publishing, Blue River Wilderness Outfitting was the location to purchase park permits for Murtle Lake. Phone (250) 673-8415 or (250) 673-0025.

Getting There: Drive east on Highway 16 to the Highway 5 junction. Take Highway 5 south through Valemount and continue south to the town of Blue River (a 5 hour drive from Prince George).

Stop in the town of Blue River and ask at the local stores where to obtain a park permit for Wells Gray Provincial Park and where to rent a canoe cart if you don't own one. Also, check on the location of firewood deposits around the lake. From Blue River, follow the signs to Murtle Lake. They will lead you on a narrow, winding logging road for 27km that ends at the trailhead parking lot to Murtle Lake. The portage trail is 2.5km long on very good trail; canoe carts work quite well.

Description: Murtle Lake is accessed by canoe/kayak only and provides wonderful interior campsites. The lake has a north and a west arm.

The north arm has steep mountainsides with many beautiful vistas, waterfalls, and generally offers more solitude than the west arm. However, it is also rainier and sees a little less sun on the beaches. The Wavy Alpine Trail near campsite #20 is a beautiful moderate to difficult day hike gaining 975m in elevation. This hike offers mountain views in all directions and a good look at the glaciers immediately to the north of the lake. Murtle River flows into the lake at the north end, meandering through a swamp. This area offers good opportunities for wildlife viewing.

The west arm is the more travelled section of the lake and is popular with families. Views are nice and the Central Mountain day hike

Paul Walsh

Camping is mostly on sandy beaches.

near campsite #10 leads to the top of Central Mountain with rewarding views (moderate to difficult 1037m elevation gain). Diamond Lagoon at the end of the west arm offers the best fishing though fish can be caught throughout the lake. Use caution near the exit of Murtle River from the lake as flows pick up fast and significant rapids are located just downstream. Hike the easy trail following the southeast side of the river down to the spectacular McDougall Falls. The round trip takes three hours. Other hikes in the west arm include Anderson Lake, File Creek/McDougall Lake, and Henrietta Lake; see the park brochure for additional information.

Camping: All campsites are superb, offering great beaches and good tent sites. The best sites in the north arm are along the west shore of the lake. The Cottonwood, Leo Island, Birch Beach and Tropicana campsites are the nicest in the west arm. If you are tight on time, the

The end of north arm as seen from Central Mountain trail.

campsites near the canoe launch at Murtle Lagoon are also very nice. You must have a permit to camp, and park rangers stationed at the Ranger Cabin on the south shore of the west arm patrol the lake to check. Most sites can accommodate more than one group, so expect neighbours. Some sites can accommodate groups of up to 10. Firewood is available, but you need to check where the firewood sites are located when registering in Blue River. All sites have bear caches and pit toilets.

Nanika Lake Chain

At a Glance: Those who like canoeing to get away from it all will really appreciate the Nanika Lake Chain. This trip avoids crowds and offers a wonderful sense of isolation.

Maps: 93-E/12, 93-E/13, 93-E/14, 93-L/3, Lakes Forest District Recreation Map, Morice Forest District Recreation Map

Getting There: From Prince George, drive west on Highway 16 to the town of Houston. Approximately 2km past Houston, turn left at the sign indicating Northwood's (Canfor's) Houston Logging Operations. Set your odometre to zero here.

Proceed for 27km on the Northwood Road (Morice Forest Service Road) until you reach a fork in the road. Take the right fork that continues up the Morice River. After another 18km, you will arrive at a second fork, just past Lamprey Creek. Take the left fork and drive past Collins Lake. At 65km from Houston just past Collins Lake turn left off the main road and follow the narrow Lamprey Forest Service Road approximately 7km to Lamprey Lake and the put-in where you can camp if you wish.

Length: 21km

Time: 2 to 3 days

Hazards: none

Best time: June to October

Description: Located about an hour's drive (72km) southwest of Houston at the end of a good gravel road, Lamprey Lake (1km long) is the first in a chain of lakes and portages that straddles the boundary between interior and coastal vegetation regions.

A short paddle along the north arm of Lamprey Lake leads straight across the lake to the first portage. It is not terribly obvious from the lake, but the first portage trailhead starts at the west edge of a logging slash and climbs into the trees. The portage to Anzac Lake is rugged (1.5km), but is compensated for by a lake full of fish and warm swimming.

Paddle southwest the 4km length of Anzac Lake and look for the next portage on the west side at the end of the lake. An old portage trail has been abandoned in favour of a newer one with a dock that is right at the end of the lake. The 500m trail to Stepp Lake is shorter and easier than the first portage.

Stepp Lake is bigger (8.5km long) than Anzac Lake so you can expect some wind. A lengthy paddle leads to some interesting lagoons and a nice campsite at the end. Before reaching the end of the lake, there are a couple of alternative campsites on the west side.

The 2km portage to Kidprice Lake is the longest and one is rewarded by the first good view of real mountains. It also has a few blueberries to occupy you while resting your canoe. The portage trail starts at the campsite at the west end of Stepp Lake. You can camp at the far end of the trail at Kidprice Lake.

Kidprice Lake (7.0km long) is colder than the others because mountain waters feed into it. It is also open, exposed and possibly windy, so you should stay close to shore. The scenic highlight of the trip is Nanika Falls in the river flowing north from Kidprice Lake. Be careful not to enter the Nanika River, as the current picks up quickly and the falls are just downstream from the lake. Park your canoe on the left bank near a fisheries shack and walk down a good trail on river left for a good view of the falls.

It is possible for fit boaters and fast canoes to paddle to the falls and back in two days, but three are recommended, especially if you want to take your time fishing, swimming and camping or exploring the upper reaches of Kidprice Lake.

Access from Kidprice Lake to Nanika Lake is difficult and seldom done.

Alternative Route: It is possible to make a loop trip by portaging around the falls and rapids and paddling down the Nanika River to Morice Lake, but this is unwise unless you have sufficient skills and the right equipment to deal with moving water and log jams. Our information on the river portion of this route has not been confirmed and the Forest Service describes this as a "wild river with large rapids and rocks and log debris which requires precise manoeuvring". They recommend the river only to expert paddlers. If you decide to try this route, refer to the Morice River trip report for access information to Morice Lake.

Camping: Camping is available on all of the lakes, Lamprey Lake, Stepp Lake, and Kidprice Lake. See the trip description for additional information. Camping is also available nearby at Morice Lake and along Morice River.

Ken Robinson

Fishing is excellent on many of the rivers and lakes in the region.

32 nation lake chain

Nation Lake Chain

At a Glance: This lake chain includes four lakes connected by meandering rivers. The scenery ranges from vistas of rolling alpine-topped mountains to flat interior plateau forests. The lakes offer good fishing and wildlife viewing with sand and gravel beaches for camping and swimming. Access to this multi-day route is relatively easy and yet the lakes provide a nice sense of remoteness.

Best time of year: mid-May to mid-October

Maps: 93-N/5, 93-N/6, 93-N/3, 93-N/2, 93-N/1, Fort St. James Forest District Recreation Map. A pamphlet showing access to, and campsites on, the Lakes is available. Call the Fort St. James Forest District (250) 996-5200, or the Fort St. James Chamber of Commerce (250) 996-7023.

Getting there: Drive from Prince George to Fort St. James by heading west on Highway 16. A few kilometres west of Vanderhoof, turn north onto Highway 27 and drive to Fort St. James.

Rating: Class 1

Length: 110km

Time: 5 to 10 days

Shuttle time: 4 hours

Hazards:
- wind and waves
- dead heads
- sweepers on rivers
- log jams on rivers
- remoteness
- waterfalls downstream of Chuchi Lake

Take-out: From Fort St. James, drive north on North Road to kilometre 100. Turn left and continue along this road for about 8km to the Chuchi Lake Forest Service Recreation Site and parking lot. This is a good take-out if you plan to paddle from west (Tsayta Lake) to east (Chuchi Lake).

Put-in: Drive north from Fort St. James along the North Road for approximately 6km; turn left onto the Tachie Highway just after the railway tracks. Around 40km turn right onto the Leo Creek Forest Service Road. At kilometre 68, continue along the Driftwood Forest Service Road. Approximately 15k along the Driftwood Road is Tchentlo Lake Lodge with access to Tchentlo Lake. To reach Tsayta Lake, the western most lake, drive to kilometre 55 of the Driftwood Road and turn right onto the Fall-Tsayta Forest Service Road. The access point is roughly 5km down this road.

An alternate route to the put-in is possible if you continue on North Road past the Chuchi Lake take out. Drive through Manson's Creek then alongside Germansen Lake until you reach the Fall Tsayta Forest Service Road. About 5km before reaching the Driftwood Forest Service Road you will reach the put-in at the west end of Tsayta Lake. This road can be quite rough.

Description: This 110km canoe route is a chain of four lakes with gentle river connections. The prevailing winds are generally from the west and the rivers flow from west to east so most people start at the west end. The chain can be broken into two separate trips with Tsayta - Indata Lakes forming one trip and Tchentlo-Chuchi Lakes forming the other. Both are enjoyable in their own right.

Tsayta and Indata Lakes are 20 and 11 kilometres long respectively. This section of the route offers views of rolling alpine-topped mountains and limestone rock cliffs. The river connecting these lakes meanders for 8 kilometres and can be quite shallow. Watch for log jams. These log jams often have a

Barbara Robertson

A beach stop on Chuchi Lake.

passageway cleared through them, but use caution and be prepared to portage. The river from Indata to Tchentlo is about 5km long.

At the west end of Tchentlo Lake is Tchentlo Lodge, which offers parking, a vehicle shuttle service and a boat launch. Tchentlo Lake is the longest lake at 45 kilometres. There is a hot spring at the west end of the lake across the bay from the lodge. Though more of a lukewarm spring, it is an interesting natural history stop nonetheless. The river between Tchentlo and Chuchi Lakes is a pleasant 5km float.

Chuchi Lake is 28 kilometres long. There are several Forest Service campsites with sandy beaches. A few of these sites are quite deluxe with cooking shelters and outhouses. Toward the end of the trip on the east end of Chuchi Lake, the bays and islands can be a bit confusing. The Forest Service campsite and parking lot are in a small bay by the north side. Nation Lakes Lodge is at the end of the chain. The shuttle service offered by this lodge is very convenient for those doing the complete route.

Camping: There are 15 Forest Service recreation campsites along the route. These have outhouses and some have cooking shelters. The use of Forest Service sites requires the purchase of a permit. Numerous other camping sites are possible though these are often very rustic and not likely to have outhouses.

Paul Walsh

Tsayta Lake has some small rocky islands to explore.

Nautley River/Nechako River

At a Glance: The Nautley River is the shortest named river in Canada. The bridge marks where Fraser Lake drains into the Nautley River and there can be some fun play at this location in high water as well as at one other location downstream on the Nechako River. In early spring during break up, come here to view Trumpeter Swans that congregate by the dozens near the bridge.

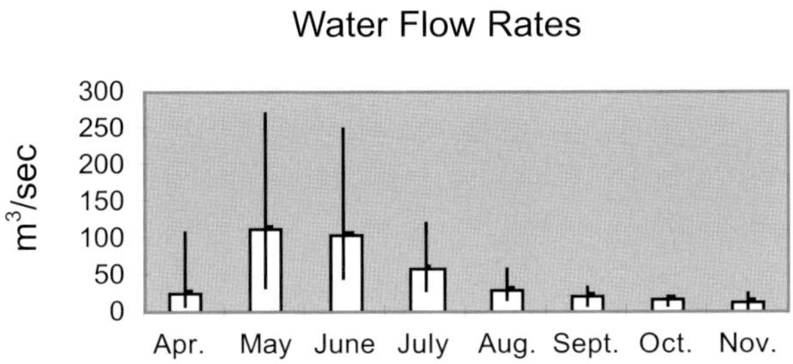

Best Time of Year: June and July. Flow rates taken near Fort Fraser.

Rating: Class 1 to 2

Length: 4km

Time: 1 hour

Shuttle time: 15 minutes

Hazards:
- log jams
- sweepers
- whirlpools

Maps: 93-K/2, Vanderhoof Forest District Recreation Map

Getting There: From Prince George, drive west approximately 135km on Highway 97 to the town of Fort Fraser. Three kilometres west of Fort Fraser turn right at Beaumont Provincial Park.

Put-in: Continue about 2km past the park to the bridge over the Nautley River, parking on the right just before the bridge. This is native reserve land and should be treated with respect.

Take-out: Continue about 4km past the bridge, staying right at any junctions. At the bottom of a hill is an old, overgrown road to the Nechako River; park here. Be sure to walk to the river to familiarise yourself with the take-out location.

Description: Below the bridge are rapids created from the foundations of an older bridge. These Class 2 rapids are fun at any water level. At high water levels, consider just parking and playing at this location. One-half kilometre downstream is the Nechako River; there is a considerable change in river volume and in temperature. Another one half kilometre later is an island that is great play spot with large eddies and a surfing wave. There is a second island downstream that also has good play opportunities. Continuing downstream, the river bends right then left. Stay on the inside corner here as there is a cave on the outside (left) bend. You can find another prime surfing wave 1km later with a big adjacent eddy on river left. When done, paddle down within the eddy as the take-out is just around the left corner.

Camping: Beaumont Provincial Park provides very nice camping on Fraser Lake with a beach.

Marian Tamkin

Running the short rapids during Vanderhoof Voyageur Days, 1995.

Nazko Lake Chain (Nazko Lake Provincial Park)

At a Glance: The Nazko Lake Chain is a small chain of six lakes interconnected by the Nazko River. This is an isolated 2 to 4 day canoe trip with short easy portages. Wildlife viewing opportunities abound.

Maps: 93-B/5, Cariboo Forest Region Recreation Map (West)

Getting There: From Prince George, drive south on Highway 97 to Williams Lake. From Williams Lake, take Highway 20 and travel west 111km to the village of Alexis Creek and go a further 8km to Bull Canyon Provincial Park. At the top of the hill past the park, turn right onto Alexis Lakes Road setting your odometre to zero. Follow the Alexis Lakes Road for 33km where it turns into Clusko-Aneko Forest Service Road. Continue on the Clusko-Aneko FSR for 12km and turn right onto a small road (1km after crossing a small bailey bridge). A campground at Loomis Lake can be seen on your right after 2km. Follow the road approximately 2km further taking the left fork in the road a short distance to a campsite and put-in on Deerpelt Lake. To skip Deerpelt Lake and the first portage, continue past Deerpelt Lake on a rough four-wheel drive road for approximately 1km to a campsite and put-in for Nazko Lake.

Rating: Class1

Length: 20km

Hazards: none

Description: The six lakes vary from shallow marsh (Nastachi Lake) to cliff walled (Tanilkul Lake). The lakes are connected by easy portage trails ranging in length from 20m to 800m. Depending on water levels, you may be able to wade your canoe down many of the small creeks connecting the lakes and avoid portages . Nazko Lake, the second in the chain, allows powerboats and is the most popular for fishing. Marshy areas in the chain provide excellent bird habitat, watch for Pelicans, and wildlife viewing is exceptionally good at Tanilkul Lake. At lower water levels some of the more marshy lakes can become impossible to navigate, particularly Nastachi Lake. Tzazati and Tchusiniltil Lakes also offer excellent fishing.

Camping: There are campgrounds at Loomis and Deerpelt lakes. Camping along the canoe chain is at unorganized sites. Look for two very nice campsites on the right shore of Tanilkul Lake.

Nechako River

At a Glance: The Nechako River runs through the Interior Plateau from its source near the Kenney Dam to its confluence with the Fraser River at Prince George. The water is dam-controlled and the seasonal flow patterns are unusual, with peak flows occurring between mid-July and late August. The river is mainly Class 1 but has several short 2 to 2+ rapids that can be lined or portaged. Wildlife is abundant and bird viewing is exceptionally good during spring and fall migration at Fort Fraser and Vanderhoof.

Rating: Class 1 to 2+

Length: total trip - 370km

Time: total trip - 1 week

Shuttle time:
•total trip 3 hours
•other sections, less than 1 hour

Hazards:
•rapidly changing water levels

There are many put-in and take-out points along the river, so it is possible to plan trips ranging from a few hours to a full week. Two very popular whitewater spots for Prince George paddlers are Isle Pierre rapids and Whitemud rapids. These trips make great afternoon or evening runs when water levels are high. Walsh Wave provides a play spot and is within city limits. Day trips for canoeists might include a run from Isle Pierre to Wilkins Park or to Cottonwood Island Park. A shorter trip from Wilkins Park to Cottonwood Park is great for an afternoon or evening paddle. A day of bird-watching might include paddling from Access #4 to Vanderhoof during spring or fall migration.

Length and time for sections:

Cheslatta Falls to Fort Fraser:	80km
Greer Creek to Fort Fraser:	53km
Fort Fraser to Vanderhoof:	57km
Vanderhoof to Prince George:	125km
Isle Pierre to Cottonwood Park:	55km

Time:
Cheslatta Falls to Fort Fraser: 2 days
Fort Fraser to Vanderhoof: 2 easy days
Vanderhoof to Prince George: 3 days

Best time of Year: mid-May to mid-October. Flow rates taken below Cheslatta Falls.

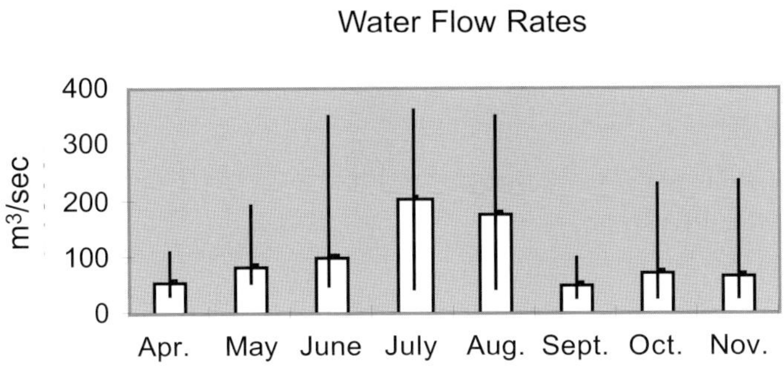

Hazards: The river is controlled by Alcan via the Skins Lake Spillway. Flows are typically very low in the spring and much higher in the summer for the sockeye salmon migration. Flow rates can, however, change dramatically in a short period of time. To anticipate the flow rates you can check in local papers for Alcan's semi-weekly report, check Alcan's web page at www.sno.net.ALCAN/, or call Alcan's Vanderhoof office.

Maps: 93-F/10, 93-F/15, 93-F/16, 93-K/2, 93-K/1, 93-J/4, 93-G/13, 93-G/14, 93-G/15 Prince George Forest District Recreation Map, Vanderhoof Forest District Recreation Map.

Getting there: There are many potential access locations on the Nechako, as a Ministry of Forests map will show, but only the most commonly used will be described here. Each of these sites allow for multi-day parking.

Put-in - Cheslatta Falls: Drive west on Highway 16 to Fort Fraser. About 2.5km before reaching Fort Fraser, turn left onto Telegraph Road. Drive for 14km and turn right on Kluskus Forest Road. Follow this road for 7km then turn right onto the Kluskus-Kenney Dam Road. In 3km turn right again onto the Kenney Dam Road. In approximately 60km you will arrive at Kenney Dam (passing access points #1 and #2 on the way). Cross the dam, veer right and in approximately 7km (200m before a bridge crosses the Cheslatta River), turn right onto a narrow, steep, dirt road on the right. This 2km road leads down to the dry Nechako canyon. It can be deeply rutted and would not be suitable for low clearance vehicles. A four-wheel-drive may be necessary to come back out.

Access #1 - Cut-off Creek: Once on the Kenney Dam Road (see put-in) drive 42km to the Cut-off Creek Recreation Site.

Access #2 - Greer Creek: Once on the Kenney Dam Road (see put-in), drive 24km to the Greer Creek Forest Recreation Site access road. This site has good campsites on the bank of the Nechako River.

Access #3 - Fort Fraser: One kilometre west of Fort Fraser a bridge crosses the Nechako River.

Access #4 - Highway 27: The bridge on Highway 27 to Fort St. James crosses the Nechako.

Access #5 - Vanderhoof: Turn north at the traffic lights onto the main street and drive a few kilometres to the bridge crossing the Nechako River.

Access #6 - Isle Pierre: Drive 35km west on Highway 16 from the junction of Highway 16 and Highway 97. Turn right onto Isle Pierre Road and drive for 11km (past the sawmill) to where the road nears the railway tracks. Turn right, cross the tracks, and drive a further 0.7km to the put-in at the old Isle Pierre ferry site.

Access #7 - Wilkins Park: Drive north on Foothills Boulevard and take the right hand exit just before a bridge crosses the Nechako River. Turn left onto Otway Road and drive up the south side of the river for approximately 13km to Wilkins Park Road. Turn right onto Wilkins Park Road and follow the signs to the boat launch in the park.

Take-out – Cottonwood Island Park: Cottonwood Island Park on River Road in Prince George.

Description: The Nechako River runs through attractive open forests of aspen, pine and spruce. Farms are also fairly common, and, of course, the river flows through the communities of Fort Fraser, Vanderhoof and Prince George. Despite frequent evidence of human settlement, the river provides many opportunities to spot mammals (black bear, moose, deer, coyote, beaver, otter), and birds (waterfowl, kingfishers, woodpeckers, eagles and osprey). Before launching your canoe, it is worth taking some time to explore the interesting rock formations in the dry Nechako canyon.

Within a few minutes of the put-in at Cheslatta Falls, you will be in a short rapid that requires manoeuvring through boulders. The river then becomes Class 1 until 16km downstream of Greer Creek, where it flows through a tight 'S' turn that ends in a Class 2 chute of standing waves. Stay river left at the first bend to avoid a mid-channel rock. Eddy out and scout. The chute is audible before you reach the 'S' turn, so as soon as you hear it, stay left. The next set of rapids is 8km further downstream and involves a 300m, Class 2 section. At higher water levels this rapid disappears. The river slows as it approaches Fort Fraser and provides a good opportunity for bird watching.

Fergus McNab

Cheslatta Falls, the new river headwaters after the building of the Kenney Dam.

A few kilometres downstream of Fort Fraser, just below the confluence of the Nechako and Nautley Rivers, are two short rapids. The first rapid has a large rock in midstream that can be run on either side. Scout this rapid before running it for the first time. The next rapid contains boulders that are fairly easy to manoeuvre. The river then becomes Class 1 until close to Braeside Ferry where it hits a head-wall on river right. Stay river left and then quickly manoeuvre to river right to avoid a rock ledge that extends 2/3 of the width of the river from the bank on river left. It is possible to paddle over the ledge in higher water levels. After passing the ledge, a sharp turn to the right takes you out of the rapid. From here to Vanderhoof, the river is Class 1 and becomes very slow. The marshes before Vanderhoof provide a stopover for migratory birds.

Downstream of Vanderhoof, the river continues to travel slowly through farm country. Benches and interesting clay and gravel cutbanks mark much of this stretch. Approximately 34km downstream from Vanderhoof, the river narrows into a short easy rapid that features riffles in high water and boulders in lower water. By now, forests have replaced the farmland and wildlife can be frequently spotted. Watch for Cluculz Creek entering on river right because the gravel bars at this confluence provide a good place to rest or camp.

The Stuart River enters 43km below Vanderhoof, and in spring and early summer it dramatically increases the volume of the Nechako. It is well worth hiking to a World Heritage Site on the west bank of the Stuart River almost within site of the confluence. This site is the location of a deserted native settlement. Signs of old habitation are not obvious in this grassy meadow, but if you are careful you can see shallow depressions in the ground that mark old food caches or building sites (see the history piece included with the Stuart River trip report).

Marian Tamkin

Voyageur Racing near downtown Prince George.

Approximately 6 kilometres before the Isle Pierre ferry site, dark basalt rocks mark the beginning of a 1km Class 2 section. The river is wide here, allowing lots of space to manoeuvre around boulders and waves. The Isle Pierre rapids begin a few kilometres downstream of the ferry site and are marked by large rocky outcrops and small islands. Run river left through the standing waves where there are many places to eddy out on the left bank. You may have to pull your boat through riffles at the top of the rapid when water levels are low. River right should be avoided, at least at the top of the rapids, because of turbulent water, whirlpools and cross-currents. See the Isle Pierre trip description for more detail.

Below Isle Pierre Rapids, the river mellows to Class 1 and continues this way until Whitemud Rapids 12km further downstream. These rapids are in two sections. The first section is Class 1+ and requires manoeuvring through boulders and standing waves. The second section is Class 2. The river bends to the right and flows over a rock ledge that extends halfway across the river from river left, causing large standing waves. Run extreme river right between the shoreline and the large flat boulder (this boulder turns into an ugly hole at higher water levels). Below these rapids the river is Class 1 to Prince George. Expect to see cut-banks and forests until you arrive in Prince George where houses line the river to the take-out.

Camping: Camping is available at Forest Service Recreation sites at Cheslatta Falls, Cut-off Creek and Greer Creek. Other sites can be found on islands and gravel bars, but these are not plentiful in high water levels. Camping is possible where Cluculz Creek and where the Stuart River flow into the Nechako. As well, one of the islands on river right in the Isle Pierre rapids is a great camping spot.

Walsh Wave

About 4km downstream of the cut-bank at the end of North Nechako Road in Prince George is a great surf wave on extreme river right, close to the only house on that side of the river. The wave can also be accessed as a park and play spot. Follow North Nechako Road West and turn left on Toombs Road. Turn left onto Walsh Road and scramble down the steep bank at the end of the road. The wave is directly across the river. The wave, which at its peak can stand around 0.5m tall, is only about 1.5m from a very strong eddy line. There is also another large rock just upstream, which can form a small pour-over at high water and can be a lot of fun in the smaller rodeo play boats. The wave is perfect for beginners because it is situated right beside an eddy and because, in the event of a swim, you can easily paddle back upstream against the slow moving water. The wave is big enough to surf tandem canoes, and kayaks can at times spin 180 degrees. If you want to paddle the Nechako solely to get to this wave, put in just after the large cut bank at the end of North Nechako Road and take out at Foothills Bridge.

35 Nechako River – Isle Pierre

At a Glance: One of the preferred runs in the Prince George area, this is a good after work outing for beginner or intermediate paddlers.

Best Time of Year: good year round. Higher water in spring, and when water is released at the Skins Spillway (often mid-July through August) are the best times for play. Check Alcan's notices regarding flow control.

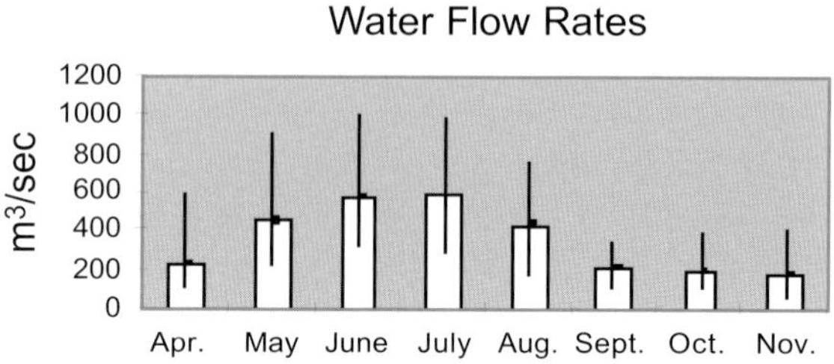

Rating: Class 2+

Length: 5km

Time: 1 hour

Shuttle time: 15 minutes

Hazards:
- river boats and jet skis
- log jams

Maps: 93-G/14, Prince George Forest District Recreation Map

Getting There: Drive west on Highway 16 from Prince George for 35.5km to the Isle Pierre Sawmill turnoff on the right. Look for the large, unique saw blade sign just after a double lane passing section returns to single lane. Follow the Isle Pierre Road for 5.5km to the sawmill. Stay left at the sawmill driving past the sawmill entrance.

Take-out: 1km past the sawmill entrance, there is a small access road on the right. Turn down this road and park. This is the closest location to the take-out. You will have to walk 400m through the sawmill site from the river back to the vehicle.

Put-in: Continue down the Isle Pierre Road for approximately 5km to a section where the road runs parallel to the railway. Turn at the road on the right that crosses the railway and follow this road a short distance to the old location of the Isle Pierre ferry.

Description: This trip is ideal for beginner paddlers as there are many large eddies and the more difficult sections can be avoided by taking sneak routes. The run begins with 1 to 2km of Class 1 moving water. Following this section is the start of the Isle Pierre Rapids, the largest rapid on the run. There is a series of rocky outcrops or small islands, creating large standing waves, boils and in some places, whirlpools. Practice your mystery moves and squirts getting plenty of vertical air time. This route can be scouted by eddying out in the monstrous eddy on river right just above the rapid and rock outcrops. If desired, beginners can almost entirely avoid the rapids by staying on river left. In extremely low water this left route may be too low to be runnable.

Downstream of this rapid, there is an island that can be run on either the left, where a surf wave sometimes forms against a cliff on river left, or on the right where a wave forms at the top of the island.

Approximately 1km downstream of this island, there is a second island that should be run on river right. Look for a surf wave on river left against a cliff wall. After this, paddle downstream for 0.5km to where you see the sawmill on river right. The take-out is located at the sawmill on river right. Look for a flagged tree along the shore at a small boulder and a trail leading up the bank. Follow this trail across the railway tracks and follow the road up the hill to the right. Walk past the office and turn right to where you see the gate where your vehicle is parked.

Camping: There is a campsite downstream of the whirlpool section on right at a rocky outcrop.

Ian Norn

The whirlpools in the first rapid provide lots of entertainment.

35 Nechako River - Whitemud Rapids

At a Glance: This park and play spot close to town can provide an evening of entertainment. It can have an amazing wide and large surf wave in the middle of the river. Be prepared to carry your boat back up for a second shot at it since it can be difficult to catch on the fly. You can also get a chance to practice your squirts, enders, and cart-wheels at certain water levels.

Best Time of Year: when the water is just at the bottom of the number 2 on the Dumas Gauge. This gauge is located on the river right pillar of the Cameron Street Bridge crossing the Nechako River in Prince George.

Maps: 93-G/14, 93-G/15, Prince George Forest District Recreation Map

Rating: Class 2+ to 3

Length: 200 meters

Time: 1 hour, or all day

Hazards:
•riverboats and jet skis
•trains

Getting There: From Prince George, drive west on Highway 16 for 16km, passing the town of Beaverly to the Mud River Valley. At the bottom of the hill descending into the valley, turn right onto Lower Mud River Road. Continue on this road, crossing a bridge over the Mud River; the road will turn to gravel. After 1km of gravel, veer right onto Chilako Station Road. Drive on Chilako Station Road for 1.3km until you see a sign indicating "no thru road." You will see Olinger Road on your right. Turn left down the cart track immediately opposite Olinger. Follow this 2-wheel drive cart track, staying right at the one road junction for 1.9km to the railroad tracks. Follow the tracks to the left for approximately 0.5km to a turnaround. From there, walk along the tracks for approximately 200m and look for flagging tape and the trailhead on the other side of the tracks. Follow this trail for 200m to the river and the rapids.

Description: This is a play spot that sometimes has a very nice ender/cart-wheel hole and frequently has a large surf wave that can provide some amazing rides. Unfortunately, you must carry your boat upstream for each attempt at the main surf wave though in lower water you can sometimes paddle up the river left shore or sneak up amongst the rock outcrops. The walk is an inconvenience, but the trail is good and very short and can be worth it for the ride! There is usually a second good wave below the main one. Once through the waves, eddy out on river right and carry your boat upstream 75 metres to the put-in eddy.

At certain higher water levels there can be a good small surf wave and an excellent hole for enders/cartwheels upstream from the put-in eddy. At very high water and very low water, play is not as good.

Camping: none.

Jeff Bailey

Surfing can be great if you can catch the wave.

Otter Attack: Terror on the Nechako

The morning of September 16 found my wife and me paddling serenely down the Upper Nechako from Cut-off Creek to Greer Creek in the fall sunshine. The afternoon before, we had driven from Prince George, leaving my trusty bicycle hidden at Greer Creek Forestry Site as a shuttle vehicle, then gone on 18km to the put in where we camped and walked nearby trails. Carol hoped to catch up on her needlework in the sun the next afternoon while I biked back up to get the van. It was to be a lazy trip on an easy river that we remembered fondly but hadn't traveled for many years.

Dawn revealed frost on the grass and fog over the river but it had burned off by the time we had doused the fire and loaded the canoe. The river was much lower than earlier years but there was lots to look at; flocks of geese and ducks, beaver, eagles, a bear in the water, and cattle here and there as the fall painted scenery drifted by.

Seeing something low and black moving on the far shore, we paddled across for a closer look. It turned out to be four otter feeding on a large spring salmon. They grunted, hissed, and snapped at each other and they tore chunks off the rotting body. Suddenly one spotted us, hissed the alarm and plunged into the water, quickly followed by the others. They then all reared from the water, scant feet away, hissing and glaring angrily, one still choking down a piece of fish. We retreated. Have you ever tried to back paddle with your hands six inches apart at the top of the shaft?

Then they moved downstream, clearly planning to cut off our escape! We went upstream past the mangled fish, and then circled out into the slowly moving current. The dark slinky creatures moved to intercept us, one hit the bottom of the canoe, and another grazed my paddle blade. Could they possibly capsize us by biting our paddles?

Then as quickly as it began they were falling behind us, still hurling abuse, as we entered fast shallow water downstream. Relief at our narrow escape expressed itself in laughter as we paddled on our way. Perhaps that's why we ran aground on a gravel bar in mid channel a short time later.

Trish Chapman

The pour over just above the main Whitemud Rapid.

The upper cut banks are a popular launch location for day tripping into Prince George.

Fergus McNab

36 Pack River

At a Glance: This trip is ideal for a relaxing canoe excursion for beginners and intermediates wanting a variety of lake and river paddling.

Best Time of Year: May to October

Maps: 93-J/14, 93-O/3, Mackenzie Forest District Recreation Map, Prince George Forest District Recreation Map

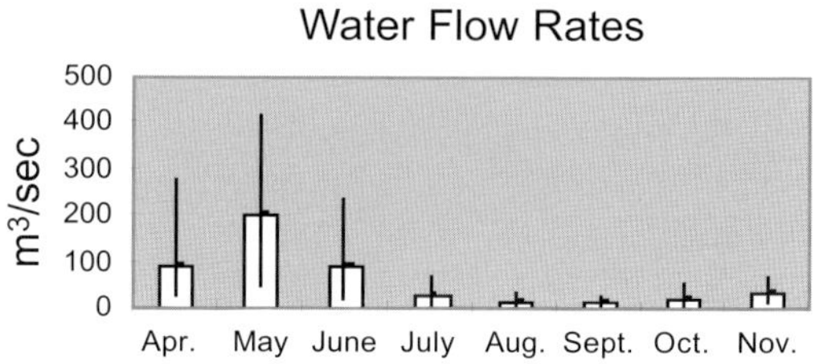

Getting There: From Prince George, drive 140km north on Highway 97 to the north end of McLeod Lake.

Rating: Class 1 to 2

Length: 18km

Time: 5 hours
shorter sections can be run

Shuttle time: 15 minutes

Hazards:
•high winds on Tudyah Lake
•sweepers

Put-in – McLeod Lake: Drop your boat in the water at the north end of McLeod Lake at the gas station/cafe on the highway. The east side of the lake and the access at the Carp Lake Road Bridge is mostly private land and the west side is primarily native reserve land so should not be used for access.

Access #1 - Pumphouse: Drive 4.5km north of McLeod Lake and turn left at the Pumphouse Road. This location can be used as either a take-out or put-in to shorten the trip.

Access #2 – Tudyah Lake: Continue north on Highway 97 for 8km to Tudyah Lake Provincial Park. Leave a vehicle at the boat launch, the location of the take-out.

Take-out: Continue north of Tudyah Lake Provincial Park for 5.5km to the Finlay/Phillip Forest Service Road on the right (just south of the Windy Point restaurant and stores). Follow this road for 8km to a bridge over the Pack River just upstream of Williston Lake. This is the take-out.

Description: Enter the river at the north end of McLeod Lake. On the way down the river, there are only a few eddies. After about 1.5 hours paddling down the river, there is a big eddy against a small, mud cut-bank on river right. Just downstream of this eddy, there is a small play wave and shortly after that on river right is the pump house. Half an hour later, the river meanders into a marshy area and a further half an hour of paddling takes you to Tudyah Lake. From the river mouth, the picnic area can be seen on the far point of land ahead on the right. This is an optional take-out location.

Rick Brine

The Pack River is a relaxing trip.

Paddling the length of Tudyah Lake takes about one hour. The river leaves the lake at the north end on the left. The first section of the river is fast flowing water with a few easy rapids; this section is excellent for fishing. Further downstream, the high water line appears from the backwater of Williston Lake. The last stretch is lazy, meandering water.

Camping: Tudyah Lake Provincial Park. Good camping is also available at the take-out.

Parsnip River

At a Glance: The Parsnip River is an easy Class 1 river that has a real wilderness feel and provides plenty of opportunity to spot a variety of birds and large mammals. There are a number of access points to the river, so trips from half a day to four days can be planned easily. A great week-long trip would involve a few days on Arctic, Portage, and Pacific Lakes before paddling north to the Highway 97 bridge near Windy Point.

Length and time for sections

Put-in to Access #1:	14km	4 hours
Access #1 to Access #2:	15km	4 hours
Access #2 to Access #3:	49km	8 hours
Access #3 to Take-out:	57km	10 hours

Best time of year: summer, when water levels are lower and camping sites are plentiful.

Maps: 93-J/15, 93-J/16, 93-O/2, 93-F/9, 93-I/12, 93-A/5, Prince George Forest District Recreation Map, Mackenzie Forest District Recreation Map (South)

Rating: Class 1

Length: total trip - 135km

Time: 4 to 7 days

Shuttle time:
total trip - 4 hours
15 to 60 minutes between adjacent access points

Hazards:
•occassional log jams
•few campspots in high water

Getting there: Drive north on Highway 97 and turn right a few kilometres south of Bear Lake town site onto a road leading to The Pas Lumber. This mill marks kilometre 0 of the 700 (Chuchinka) Road. Three of the five access points to the river are on the 700 Road. Trips on the Parsnip can be planned between any two of the five access points.

Put-in: The most upstream put-in is at kilometre 786 of the 700 Road. From The Pas Lumber, follow the 700 Road to kilometre 755 where the road veers south (right) to follow the general course of the river. At kilometre 777, the road crosses the Parsnip (Access

#1). Continue on to kilometre 786 staying right at a Y in the road at approximately kilometre 784.

Access #1: Kilometre 777 (see above)

Access #2: At the junction near kilometre 755, stay straight until a bridge crosses the Parsnip River.

Access #3: This put-in is located on the 800 Road, which can be accessed by turning left at kilometre 714 of the 700 Road. Continue on this road until you reach a major T-intersection at kilometre 828. Turn right and continue past Tacheeda Lakes to kilometre 848, where you will see a small dirt road leading to a boat launch. Tacheeda Lakes and the 800 Road can also be accessed by turning right 15km north of Bear Lake. An information stand can be seen at the junction of Highway 97 and the Tacheeda Lakes road.

Take-out: The last take-out on the Parsnip River is on Highway 97 at the bridge between Windy Point and Mackenzie Junction.

Description: The upper segment of the Parsnip River meanders down a valley with scenic mountain vistas to the east and west (from put-in to Access #2). It is a small volume river that wends its way north through marshy ground overgrown with alders. Occasionally, evergreen forests line the river.

After the confluence of Chuchinka Creek, the Parsnip becomes noticeably larger and for several kilometres various islands provide good resting spots. Then the river suddenly slows and meanders, the islands disappear and the river channel weaves its way through willow lined banks. Long ox-bow corners allow you to see many things twice. Downstream of the junction with the Hominka River, the Parsnip seems much larger but continues to meander slowly. It picks up speed again near the Table River and the vegetation along the river is predominantly evergreen forests, with occasional cottonwood stands. The faster flowing current and evergreen-lined banks continue along the lower Parsnip from Access #3 to the take-out on Highway 97.

Camping: Camping is possible at each of the put-ins. The first campsites downstream of the put-in are located between access points #1 and #2 at two old cabin sites, both on river right. A third possible campsite is on a gravel bar where the Chuchinka Creek flows into the Parsnip on river left. Downstream of Access #2, at lower water levels (typically mid-July through fall), there are plenty of campsites on gravel bars, except in the area where the Hominka River flows into the Parsnip. At higher water levels, camping on gravel bars is not possible, but sites can be found in the dry, open, evergreen forests that line the river.

James Taylor

Fog adds mystery to this wilderness trip on the Parsnip

Pine River - East Pine to Taylor

At a Glance: The canyon at the upper portion of the trip is very large and the black rock walls intriguing. When combined with other portions of the Murray River, this river can end a nice wilderness trip with few hazards for less experienced paddlers.

Maps: 93-P/11, 93-P/14, 94-A/2, 94-A/3, Dawson Creek Forest District Recreation Map

Getting There: From Prince George, drive north to Chetwynd and continue east on Highway 97 to the town of East Pine.

Put-in: East Pine Provincial Park in the town of East Pine.

Take-out: Along the Alaska Highway north of Fort St. John at the town of Taylor. Taylor Landing Provincial Park is located on the Peace River at the town of Taylor. Reach the park by turning right just before the bridge spanning the Peace. When travelling by boat, the landing is on river right of the Peace River 400m downstream of the Alaska Highway bridge crossing the Peace.

Rating: Class 1 to 2

Length: 88km

Time: 2 days

Shuttle time: 2 hours

Hazards:
•canyon with short ledges

Description: A medium to large volume river, the Pine flows at a relatively brisk and consistent pace with a few lake-like slower sections. The river is narrow and scenic for the first 3 to 4km downstream of the put-in, running through a steep rock-walled canyon. In this section, watch for larger haystacks and ledges stretching out from the river left canyon walls. Afterward, the river widens and the landscape opens up into the Peace country. The occasional farm reaches the bank of the river.

Camping: Approximately 20km from the take-out, camping is available at Charlie Lake or Kiskatinaw Provincial Parks. Along the river, camping is unorganized and somewhat scarce on gravel bars. Note that camping is not available at the put-in at East Pine Prov. Park.

Puntchesakut Lake Provincial Park

At a Glance: A popular destination for Quesnel families.

Maps: 93-B/15, Cariboo Forest Region Recreation Map (East)

Getting There: From Prince George drive south on Highway 97 to the City of Quesnel. Cross the Fraser River on the Moffat Bridge into West Quesnel and drive 40km west via the Nazko Road to the park.

Description: Paddlers will seek this lake if they are interested in fishing for large trout in the spring. The beach access makes it appropriate for family trips as well.

Camping: There is no camping in the park.

Length: 5km

Hazards:
powerboats

James Taylor

The Northwest Brigade Paddling Club offers fun pool sessions in winter.

Purden Lake

At a Glance: Purden Lake has something for almost everyone. A sandy public beach draws sunbathers and motor boaters. Big fish draw fishers, and clear water coupled with undeveloped shoreline draws canoeists.

Best time of year: mid-May to mid-October, but if you are looking for warm water wait until July and hope for the best!

Maps: 93-H/13, Prince George Forest District Recreation Map. For information contact BC Parks Prince George Office, Box 2045 (4051 18th Ave.), Prince George, BC, V2N 2J6. Telephone: (250) 565-6340.

Length: 7km

Time: 1 easy day

Hazards:
- powerboats
- jet skis

Getting there: Starting at the junction of Highways 97 and 16, drive east on Highway 16 for approximately 60km. Turn left at the sign directing you to Purden Lake Provincial Park. Drive a further 2.5km to the boat launch.

Description: The best place to put-in is the boat launch located at the west end of the lake. The public beach is on the north shore 1km away. Picnic tables, sandy beaches and change houses provide a perfect spot on a hot day for you and many other beach enthusiasts. The area around the public beach can be busy with boats and jet skis, but it is fairly easy to escape this excitement by paddling toward the northeast end of the lake. Small bays along the undeveloped north shore are suitable for swimming. These bays don't offer very good beaches, but the water is clear and invites you to take a quick dip on a hot day. The bays also provide opportunities to practice kayak or canoe rolling in clear, warm water. Islands at the northeast end of the lake, 4 to 5km from the public beach, are good destinations, the smaller island having an excellent picnic site. Expect fishing boats almost anywhere on the lake.

Camping: Camping is available in the provincial park, but the park's popularity requires you make reservations well in advance.

Quesnel River

This medium volume river flows swiftly through most sections, including several Class 4 canyons. There are many access points on the river, so either day trips or multi-day trips can be planned.

There are two sections of interest for advanced (The Upper) and intermediate (The Lower) level paddlers looking for great play and river running. Two good day tripping sections of the river for beginner and intermediate canoeists are also described: the section from Beaver Mouth Creek to the Gravelle Bridge and the section from below the Lower Quesnel run to the City of Quesnel. The section of the river from Quesnel Forks to Beaver Mouth Creek is not included as a separate trip description, but it is Class 1 to 2 with few hazards. See the Beaver Mouth Creek to Gravelle Bridge trip report.

John Marien

A raft pulled out just above Vic and Oly's Canyon on the Beaver Mouth Creek section.

Quesnel River - Upper

At a Glance: This is a world-class run. It has wonderful surf waves, play holes, long continuous rapids, strong turbulent sections, and some pushy sections. Most of the run is Class 3 with three Class 4 drops and one Class 4+ drop to end the canyon run called the Devil's Eyebrow. Some other features that make it worthy are the clear water flowing out of huge Quesnel Lake; the salmon run from July to October, easily viewed from the bridge and on the water. As well, since the water flows out of a lake, it is slightly warmer than many other rivers of this region.

Best Time of Year: lower and medium water levels offer better opportunities for play boating, mid-July to October

Maps: 93-A/12, Cariboo Forest Region Recreation Map (East)

Getting There: From Prince George, drive 188km south on Highway 97 to the town of McLeese Lake. When entering the town adjacent to the lake, turn left onto Beaver Lake Road at the signs indicating Gibraltar Mines and Likely. Follow this road for 3km climbing a steep hill and then veer right onto Beaver Lake Road just past the power lines, following the signs to Likely and Horsefly. Follow Beaver Lake Road (gravel) for approximately 30km to its end at the road leading to Likely. Turn left at the highway and follow it for approximately 35km to the town of Likely.

Put-in: At the salmon containment area on river right just below the bridge spanning the river in Likely or at the lake across from the hotel.

Take-out: A well-maintained forestry road leads to the take-out at the historic Quesnel Forks. It is about 15km from the bridge in Likely. After crossing the bridge, continue up the hill. Turn left at the first opportunity and follow the signs to Quesnel Forks. Stay left at all junctions. The best take-out is now just past the old cemetery. There has been tremendous erosion at the lower take-out over the past couple years due to a huge landslide just upstream.

Rating: Class 3+ to 4+

Length: 10km

Time 1 hour

Shuttle time: 20 minutes

Hazards:
strong hydraulics

Description: At the start of the run just below the bridge, there are some great play holes and waves caused by the collapse of an earlier bridge. At certain levels, if you wanted, you could park and play here for hours without heading downstream.

Below here, the first half of the run is punctuated with some steeper drops containing large waves, but they are clean and do not need to be scouted. After the finish of a long rapid, about 1km long, you will get a short breather and will see large cliffs ahead on the left. This marks the approach to the Bullion Pit (named after an old mine). You will first pass through a section of huge standing waves and then some powerful hydraulics along the cliffs. Just past here is a large eddy on your right. This is a good place to regroup or have lunch, and it marks the halfway point of the run.

After this point on the river, there are a few accelerating wavy rapids and plenty of play spots before the Devil's Eyebrow. The name is derived from the natural stone arch located just above the tightest, and at times the gnarliest, section of the run. Look up if you have the time! If it is your first run

Wayne Giles

Ripping it up in Deep Throat, the hole leading down to the Devil's Eyebrow.

on this section, scout this rapid. You will recognize it when the river drops very steeply through a constricted, long canyon section. Take out on the left. Portaging this drop is possible, but it is not one most people would want to do. The entrance to the Eyebrow is marked by a large hole, Deep Throat. Following this, the water is turbulent. The section ends with a tight S-turn to the right where water hits a headwall and causes strange hydraulics; the stone arch is located immediately above. This is the last major rapid on the run and is about 2km upstream of the take-out.

Wayne Giles

Darkside, one of the great spots to spend an hour.

Camping: The site of Quesnel Forks, located at the confluence of the Cariboo and Quesnel Rivers, is a designated B.C. Forestry campground. As such, there is a user fee for each night spent there that is charged to the many summertime campers that come to this popular site. Camping is excellent on the site of this historic gold-mining city. Campers and souvenir seekers have looted the town for artifacts and scavenged pieces of the buildings for firewood. Please respect this site and leave it as you found it.

Quesnel River – Beaver Mouth Creek to Gravelle Bridge

At a Glance: An excellent day trip close to the City of Quesnel along a scenic, wilderness section of the river. There are some good practice locations for eddy turns, a short canyon section and some standing waves.

Best Time of Year: medium to low water, usually in August or September. There are powerful hydraulics in the canyon section at higher water.

Maps: 93-B/9, 93-B/16, Cariboo Forest Region Recreation Map (East)

Getting There: From Prince George, drive 115km south on Highway 97 through Quesnel. Travel across the Quesnel River. Turn left at the gas station onto the Quesnel Hydraulic Road at the top of the long hill.

Rating: Class 2

Length: 19km

Time: 5 to 6 hours

Shuttle time: 45 minutes

Hazards:
- log jams
- sweepers
- ledge 1.2km from put-in

Take-out: Drive approximately 25km on the Quesnel Hydraulic Road to the turnoff to the Gravelle Bridge. Turn left and drive 500m down to Gravelle Bridge. Take out on river left downstream of the bridge.

Put-in: Continue driving another 17km from the Gravelle Bridge turnoff to the bridge crossing Beaver Creek. You can put in either in Beaver Creek, which flows into the Quesnel River 100m downstream, or on the left just before the bridge crossing. Another possibility is to drive across the bridge and turn left into a forestry campsite on the Quesnel River.

Alternate Put-in: If you wish to paddle from Quesnel Forks down to Beaver Mouth Creek see the Upper Quesnel trip description for access information from Quesnel Forks. Jet boats often access the portion of the river downstream from Quesnel Forks to fish. Quesnel Forks to Beaver Mouth Creek could be combined with Beaver Mouth Creek to Gravelle Bridge for a multi-day, Class 1 to 2, intermediate canoe trip.

Description: This section is mostly a Class 1 paddle interspersed with some Class 2 water. There is a ledge extending into the river from river right approximately 1.2km downstream of the put-in. Scout from the river left shore. There is a route through on the extreme river left. The ledge can be portaged or lined from river right. After the ledge, the river continues as Class 1. Approximately 6km downstream of the ledge there is a 2.5km stretch of the river with excellent eddies for turning practice. Following this is Vic and Oly's Canyon. The river bends to the right, and you can see the canyon ahead where the river narrows. Scout the canyon from river right. The canyon is considered Class 2+ at higher water levels. There are good shoreline eddies throughout the canyon and possible large standing waves with tricky eddy-lines. The canyon can be run down the centre. After the canyon, the river is Class 1 to the take-out.

Camping: Unorganized at the put-in and take-out. Camping is limited along the river.

John Marien

Scouting the first ledge on the Beaver Mouth section.

41 Quesnel River - Lower

At a Glance: The staple run for paddlers in the City of Quesnel, this run has plenty of play spots at different water levels and offers great scenery. In high water, this run becomes very pushy and experienced boaters will enjoy the huge haystacks and boiling hydraulics.

Best Time of Year: medium to high water levels

Maps: 93-B/16, Cariboo Forest Region Recreation Map (East)

Getting There: From Prince George, travel south on Highway 97 through the town of Hixon. Approximately 40km after Hixon, you will cross the Cottonwood River Bridge. Note your odometre reading here. 3.5km past the Cottonwood River Bridge look for McLean Road on your left (approximately 100km south of Prince George). Turn left on McLean Road (Schemanauer Road) and follow it for 7km to its end at Highway 26 (the Barkerville Highway). Turn left on Highway 26 and follow it for 7km looking for a new, metal-gated, gravel road on the right at the top of a small hill.

Rating: Class 3 to 4

Length: 4km

Time: 2 hours

Shuttle time: 15 minutes

Hazards:
- log jams
- floating logs
- strong hydraulics

Note: Access past the gate down this road has changed frequently in the past few years. A mine was operating down the road and controlling access but has since gone out of business. The gate has been open recently but might again be locked and access controlled at some future date.

Put-in: Enter the gate and follow this road down to the valley bottom near the river. At the mining site on the right (gravel pit) at the bottom, look for a T-junction with a smaller road heading straight ahead. Follow this smaller road for 300m to a clearing by the river where you can park.

Take-out: Return to the mining site and T-junction and follow the road that heads to the right through the mining site (gravel pit). Follow this four-wheel drive only road until it ends at a clearing/campsite by the river.

Alternate Route to Take-out: Two wheel drive vehicles can approach the take-out. From the junction on Highway 97 and Highway 26, travel 5 to 6km up Highway 26 to the Quesnel Canyon Road on the right (approximately 4km before McLean Road/Schemanauer Road intersects Highway 26). Bear right and drive until the road is impassable at the top of a hill overlooking the river and the campsite located at the take-out. You will have to carry your boats up the steep hill back to the vehicles.

Description: Depending on water levels, one of the best play spots is located at the put-in. At high water levels, a large surf wave forms that is green nearer the shore, with a foam pile towards the centre. You can park and play here for hours, surfing and spinning, without even running the rest of the river as at this level much of the other features are washed out. However, at lower levels this spot becomes more of a hole, and you will want to head down river to catch the other play spots.

A long straight section, containing numerous play waves and eddies, precedes the next drop where the river bends to the left. Avoid the huge waves in the centre by staying river right through a rock garden or, for more skillful paddlers, by creeping down the left shore eddies below the cliff. Another excellent surf wave, called Roadside, forms on river left at medium and lower water levels. It is also possible to park and play at this wave since the road is adjacent to the river directly across from the wave.

Below Roadside the river again calms. Watch for a cabin on river right at a right bend in the river. There is an excellent surfing wave on river left across from the cabin at high water levels called Cabin Surf though you may need a longer boat (greater than 8 feet) to catch it.

The degree of difficulty of the river increases after Cabin Surf. The river splits around an island with both the left and right channels hitting headwalls on the riverbank cliff as they converge together past the islands. The left channel is the recommended route around the island; at low water, the right channel has a keeper that extends to the centre from the left shore. These channels should be scouted before running them. The right channel can be scouted from shore, but the left channel can only be scouted from the island.

Below the island the river bends left with high cliffs on river left and large rocks and a beach on river right. There is an excellent play wave in this stretch called Mermaid. This is the last play spot before the canyon.

At high water levels, the canyon is very swift with huge waves and fierce boils on river left. It is best run between the boils on river left and the huge waves centre left. At low water levels, you must approach the canyon from right of centre to avoid a rocky ledge stretching halfway across the river from the left and then ferry left to avoid two large holes on the right half of the river.

The canyon spills out into large boiling eddies; watch for the take-out on river right near the picnic site. If you miss the take-out, you will drop through large waves left of an island. These waves are the last rapids on the river before Quesnel, which is considerably further downstream.

Camping: Camping at the take-out is excellent at an old Forest Service Site. However, this site can only be accessed using four-wheel drive vehicles. There is a good campground with a sandy beach at Ten Mile Lake Provincial Park 5km south of the Cottonwood River Bridge on Highway 97, 1km south of the McLean Road turnoff.

Paul Walsh

The wave at the put-in at prime water levels.

Quesnel River – Lower Quesnel to Quesnel

At a Glance: This is nice float trip with gently moving water located very near the City of Quesnel. A great day trip through some scenic stretches of river.

Best Time of Year: anytime after spring flood

Maps: 93-B/16, Cariboo Forest Region Recreation Map (East)

Getting There: From Prince George, travel south on Highway 97 through the town of Hixon. Approximately 40km after Hixon, you will cross the Cottonwood River Bridge. Note your odometre reading here. 3.5km past the Cottonwood River Bridge look for McLean Road on your left (approximately 100km south of Prince George). Turn left on McLean Road (Schemanauer Road) and follow it for 7km to its end at Highway 26 (the Barkerville Highway). Turn left on Highway 26 and follow it for 7km looking for a new, metal-gated, gravel road on the right at the top of a small hill.

Rating: Class 2

Length: 15km

Time: 5 to 6 hours

Shuttle time: 45 minutes

Hazards:
•log jams
•sweepers

Note: Access past the gate down this road has changed frequently in the past few years. A mine was operating down the road and controlling access but has since gone out of business. The gate has been open recently but might again be locked and access controlled at some future date.

Put-in: Enter the gate and follow this road down to the valley bottom near the river. At the mining site on the right (gravel pit) at the bottom, follow the road that heads to the right through the mining site (gravel pit). Follow this four-wheel drive road until it ends at a clearing/campsite by the river.

Alternate Route to Put-in: Two-wheel drive vehicles can get to the put-in. From the junction on Highway 97 and Highway 26, travel 5 to 6km up Highway 26 to the Quesnel Canyon Road on the right (approximately 4km before McLean Road/Schemanauer Road intersects Highway 26). Bear right and drive until the road is impassable at the top of a hill overlooking the river and the campsite located at the put-in. You will have to carry your boats down the steep hill to the river.

Take-out: Drive south on Highway 97 to Quesnel. Highway 97 turns into Front Street in downtown Quesnel and runs adjacent to the Fraser River. Continue straight on Front Street past Carson Avenue and look for an entrance to Ceal Tingley Park, the first right past Carson Avenue. The park is located at the junction of the Fraser and Quesnel River. On the river, the take-out to the park will be on river right. Use caution when approaching the bridge pylons at Quesnel.

Description: Immediately below the put-in there is a Class 3 rapid. This rapid has more to it than it appears from shore, so putting in below it or lining on river right is the best option. Below this, the river slows to Class 1 to 2 all the way to Quesnel. The river travels through some remote stretches before becoming more populated along its banks. Swimming and fishing can be good, making for a nice day trip in the canoe. Look for the take-out at the last railway bridge just before the Fraser River. Carry your boat 150m to your car at Ceal Tingley Park.

Camping: Camping at the put-in is excellent at an old Forest Service Site. However, this site can only be accessed using four-wheel drive vehicles. There is a good campground with a sandy beach at Ten Mile Lake Provincial Park 5km south of the Cottonwood River Bridge on Highway 97, 1km south of the McLean Road turnoff.

All's well that ends in Wells

September 13, 1991 was a Friday. Too bad for Ed. That was the day he decided to organize a "discreet trip" on the Quesnel Canyon. Ed hates crowds. Ed hates chaos. He prefers nice, tight, little bands of well-organized amigos who quietly show up on time, with all their gear. He doesn't like to fight for space in the eddies. He would rather surf than chase swimmers. He particularly hates complicated shuttles. So when Ed disclosed his discreet trip, he only called a couple of people, and he was careful to use the word "discreet" at least three times in his invitation.

Two days later at 8:00 A.M. sharp, Ed nursed his coffee in the shadow of Mr. P.G. Madcap mayhem muddied his morning. A dozen paddlers, including two (ughh!) open-boaters, damned his dawn awakening. Excitement ran high - far too high for what should have been a mellow morning. Boats and vehicles and boaters and gear danced in the dust.

One of the throng was a new guy named Ernie. Ernie had a big truck; just right for gearbags and paddles and a pile of boats. Being a nice guy, Ernie opened his mouth, and they honoured his offer by tossing tons of gear into the back of his truck. One generous soul offered to ride with Ernie to show him the way to the River. Ernie politely declined and said he'd follow along. Everybody else piled into vehicles and tore off down the highway. Determined to set land speed records, they ripped past Ernie, who enjoyed the sunrise at a sedate and legal speed.

As usual, paddlers arrived at the river, jumped out of their trucks and into their gear. Ed hoped that he could be really efficient and put in before the crowd. Soon, they were all dressed up but had no place to go. You see, Ernie had most of the boats and paddles and he must have been driving awfully slowly because he hadn't shown up yet.

Paddlers started to burn. "Where the hell is Ernie?" There was only enough gear for a couple of boaters to paddle. A heated, philosophical debate ensued about the ethics of splitting up the group. One paddler jumped into his boat and ferried back and forth at the take-out. Another paced furiously, ruminating about the shuttle part of a recent trip leadership course.

Time dragged on. Anger turned to concern. "Where the hell is Ernie?" People jumped into vehicles and started driving up and down the highways and biways. Ed started walking. People scouted backroads and scoured the ditches for Ernie's overturned truck. Ed kept walking. People drove into Quesnel and out towards Barkerville. Ed kept walking. People saw Ed walking and offered him a ride. Ed kept walking.

Where the hell was Ernie? Did he think all that gear was worth stealing? Did he drive to Mexico? Was he lying in a heap of broken paddles in the ditch near Hixon?

Frustrated and concerned, they gave up on paddling and went home. Where the hell was Ernie? Well, it seems that he was somewhere near Wells, about 80 km upstream from the canyon. It seems that he missed the little sign that said "Quesnel Canyon Road" and just kept driving. After several hours of watching the sunrise, it occurred to him that maybe he should turn off the highway. Then he got a flat tire and had some trouble changing it because he didn't have a jack and the truck was rather heavy with all that paddling gear in the back. He then decided to survey all the logging roads between Wells and Quesnel, arriving back at the main highway late in the afternoon. Still hoping to connect with all his new paddling friends, he waited patiently in Quesnel for another three hours before turning home. He arrived in Prince George around 8:00 P.M. and continued driving north. He's probably in Inuvik by now.

Wonder if Ed got there first...?

Raush River

At a Glance: This easy paddling river trip offers spectacular scenery in a pristine wilderness environment. Load up your canoes for a day or overnight trip and watch the scenery while floating by.

Best Time of Year: anytime after spring flood. Note that because this river is heavily glaciated in the headwaters, water levels can fluctuate considerably over a day, depending on temperatures.

Maps: 83-E/4, 93-H/1, Robson Valley Forest District Recreation Map

Getting There: From Prince George, travel east 200km on Highway 16 to the town of McBride. Continue east on Highway 16 for 30km, and turn right on the road leading across the Fraser River to the town of Dunster.

Put-in: After crossing the Fraser River, turn left at the T-junction to the general store and continue southeast towards Tete Jaune, on the back road. Take the right fork at about 12km from the highway onto the Forest Service Road. Stay on the main road and cross Kiwa Creek at about 24km from the highway. Then turn right on the logging road, which parallels the creek. Follow the main road to km 29 and take the right fork. Continue on about 1km into the logging block to a trail-head sign at the end of the road. This is in the pass between the Kiwa and Raush, about 1100ft above the Raush River. The trail down is about 2km long and fairly well marked. It follows an ATV trail for about 1km, then branches off left to a foot trail. The foot trail portion has been cut out, but it might be difficult for longer boats and would definitely not accommodate wheeled carriers. The ATV route can be travelled further with wheels but goes a considerable distance before accessing the river. Please note that there are cattle grazing on Crown Land in the Kiwa and on a small amount of private land in the lower Raush. Please respect the owners' property and animals.

Rating: Class 2

Length:
•32km on Raush
•10km on Fraser

Time: 8 to 10 hours

Shuttle time: 2 hours

Hazards:
•sweepers

Take-out: From McBride, take Highway 16 for 8km east to Hinkleman Road and turn right. About 2.5km after crossing the Holmes River, turn right through an unlocked gate into an open cattle-grazing area (public land). Stay to the right and follow a track until a power line is encountered. Turn left and follow the power line to the river.

Alternate Take-out: At the Highway 16 Bridge at McBride.

Description: Flowing from the Premier Range of the Cariboo Mountains, the Raush River enters the Fraser River between Dunster and McBride. It is the largest undeveloped, unprotected watershed in 'southern' British Columbia. This portion of the river slowly meanders through a magnificent wilderness setting. Just prior to joining the Fraser River, there is approximately 0.5km of faster moving Class 2 water.

Camping: Unorganized along the river or at the put-in or take-out. In addition, there are numerous forest service sites in the region.

First Descent

A first descent of the entire river was done in 1999 by four kayakers led by Robert Beaudry, an Adventure Guide Instructor at University College of the Cariboo in Kamloops. They were joined later in the trip by marathon swimmer Fin Donnelly, who swam the lower half of the river, and a support crew of whitewater rafts and canoes. This was an expensive access, requiring the use of helicopters. The expedition was organized to draw attention to the quality wilderness in the Raush and promote its protection.

The upper half is primarily Class 4 and 5 water and provided a considerable challenge and thrill to the four accomplished kayakers who made the voyage. The river calms considerably after Black Martin Creek, where canoes become an option (but access is still a major problem). Downstream of the Black Martin confluence, almost the entire length of the river is made up of slow meanders in a magnificent wilderness setting.

Michael Bouris

Some action on the river above Black Martin Creek.

Salmon River

The Salmon River runs southwest through the Interior Plateau, from northwest of Carp Lake to the Fraser River just north of Prince George. The upper reaches of the river are largely unexplored by canoeists, and the section just upstream of Highway 97 is rarely paddled because of log jams. The section between Highway 97 and the railway bridge, a few kilometers before the confluence with the Fraser, provides a nice Class 2 run that would be great for an afternoon or evening run in higher water levels.

Ken Robinson

A typical scene on the Salmon River

600 Road Bridge to Highway 97

At a Glance: This river is small and intimate, being only 20m wide at the put-in. Lush vegetation lines the banks and supports a large variety of bird life. Many marshy areas provide great wildlife viewing and gravel bars provide resting and camping spots. Unfortunately the last half of this section often has large log jams that are difficult to portage because of the lush vegetation. Almost no one canoes this river because of log jams, even though it is otherwise a very appealing river.

Best Time of Year: late May to mid-July

Maps: 93-J/6, 93-J/3, 93-J/2, 93-J/7, Prince George Forest District Recreation Map

Getting There: Drive north on Highway 97 to the Salmon River Bridge.

Rating: Class 1 to 2

Length:
- 600 Rd to Moldowan Rd 24km
- Moldowan Rd to Hwy 97 54km

Time:
- 600 Rd to Moldowan Rd 5 hours
- Moldowan Rd to Hwy 97 1.5 days

Shuttle time: 2 hours

Hazards:
- sweepers
- log jams
- dangerous in high water

Take-out: Park on the north side of the Highway 97 bridge at a pull-out on the left hand side. It is also possible to park at the campground just downstream of the bridge if you ask the attendant.

Access #1: Turn onto Chief Lake Road either from Highway 97 north, or from Foothills Boulevard. From the intersection of Foothills and Chief Lake Road drive 10.6km and turn right onto Nukko Lake road. In 12.2km turn right onto the 200 Road. Turn right again in approximately 15km onto the 400 Road. Within 2km turn right onto the 600 Road. The bridge crossing the Salmon River is 500m from this intersection. To access a parking and camping area next to the bridge, turn right about 300m after the intersection.

Access #2:
From the intersection of Chief Lake Road and Foothills Boulevard, drive 2.5km and turn right onto Pilot Mountain Road. In approximately 17km veer right onto Moldowan Road. This road leads to the river in approximately 5km. Be aware that the bridge that used to cross the Salmon River has been removed and access to the river might be difficult.

Description: The river at the put-in is small and slow moving andlined with evergreen forests. Within a few kilometers the current becomes faster, and there are some riffles and rocks to maneouver around. There is not much evidence of log jams on this section (these begin after the river takes a southerly course approximately 30kms upstream of Highway 97). Because the river is narrow, you are always close to both shores and have the opportunity to spot and hear many birds. Large gravel bars are fairly common on corners and invite you to spend a pleasant interval swimming or fishing.

The river slows for a time, and rocks and riffles disappear. The vegetation changes to predominantly alder and cottonwood trees. The river does speed up again, and the last half of the trip you can expect a series of Class 2 boulder gardens that require some manoeuvering. A large, ugly hole on river right a few hours upstream of Highway 97 should be avoided. An earlier report of this river suggested predominantly Class 1 water with one Class 2 boulder garden. This was not our experience, so we have to assume that the river looks very different in different water levels. The log jams change with each spring flood, so do not rely on previous years' experience. Every bend should be assessed for a safe passage and, if at all unsure, it should be scouted from shore.

Camping: Many gravel bars provide good camping spots

Highway 97 to Railway Bridge

At a Glance: This is a fairly short section that could be done easily in 2-3 hours. At moderate water levels there are a number of features that would provide good paddling for novices who are experienced enough to avoid possible log jams.

Best Time of Year: late May to mid-July

Maps: 93-J/2, Prince George Forest District Recreation Map

Getting There: Drive north on Highway 97 to the Salmon River Bridge.

Take-out: Turn right just after crossing the Salmon River Bridge onto Salmon Valley Road. Drive approximately 8km, and just before crossing the railway tracks turn right onto a small road that parallels the track.

Put-in: Park on the north side of the Highway 97 bridge at a pull-out on the left hand side. It is also possible to park at the campground just downstream of the bridge, if you ask the attendant.

Rating: Class 1 to 2

Length: 9km

Time: 3 hours

Shuttle time: 10 minutes

Hazards:
•sweepers
•log jams
•dangerous in high water

Description: The river in this section is lined with Cottonwood stands, and it is common to see wildlife. There are less log jams compared to the section above Highway 97; however, this stretch can also be dangerous at spring run-off due to log jams and tight bends. There are some good surf waves at moderate water levels. It is possible to continue past the railway bridge to the Fraser and to take out at any access point on the Fraser. Shelley is the most likely take out spot and is 12km from the railway bridge. Low water levels in the Salmon River are not an indication of water levels in the Fraser. You may encounter high water and strong headwinds on the Fraser River. The rating for this trip is Class 1 after the water drops to summer levels.

Camping: Camping is possible at the campsite at the put-in. Approximately 4km downstream there is a large clearing on river left that would provide many tent sites. Camping would also be possible on gravel bars when the water levels are low to moderate.

Barbarous Hydrocephalus

It's August. It's sunny. It's hot. The salmon are running on the Quesnel River. So are a bunch of happy kayakers. One of them is Dr. Bob, a well-known Licensed Fermenter of Weeds & Berries.

The kayakers crawl out of the river at the take-out, feeling fine with the glow of a good afternoon run. As they peel off their wetsuits, Dr. Bob yells, "Hey you guys, gimme a hand."

They find him half naked, crawling around in the bushes on his hands and knees, muttering something like "This is berberis aquafolium! It's really good for you! Make sure you get the roots."Before long, four more kayakers are crawling around wearing the knees out of their wetsuits and yarding up lengths of Oregon grape root and piling them in a heap.

In a frenzy, Dr. Bob yells, "Blueberries!" and stuffs an Oregon grape into his mouth. Somebody points our that he just ate an Oregon grape, not a blueberry. He spits it out and starts laughing hysterically.

At this point, a burly, bearded fisherman strolls along, rod in one hand, Kokanee beer in the other. Arriving at the scene, he stops and asks, "What are you guys doing?" Dr. Bob, ever so quick, stands up, stuffs a dirty piece of root in the fisherman's face and announces proudly, "Berberis aquafolium! It's a really good diuretic."

"Oh." The fisherman walks away, just a little faster than he arrived.

Stellako River

At a Glance: A world class fishing river, the Stellako River has beautiful, clear water with boulder gardens and standing waves, as well as some flat-water sections. Take along your bathing suit and fishing rod as there are lovely inviting pools on the way down.

Water Flow Rates

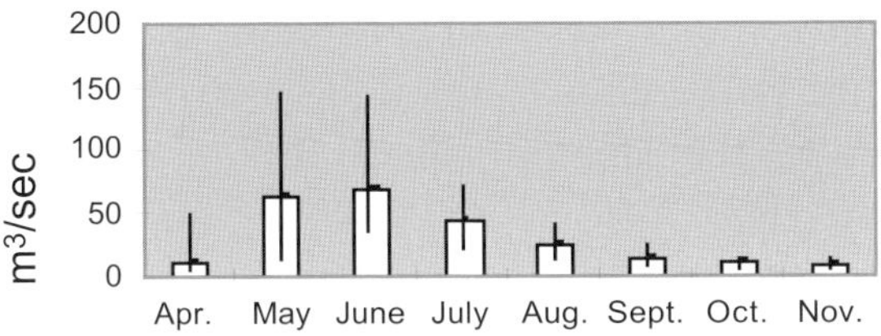

Best Time of Year: mid-June to July. Flow rates taken at Glennannan Creek.

Maps: 93-K/2, 93-K/3, Lakes District Forest Recreation Map

Getting There: From Prince George, drive 160km west on Highway 16 to the town of Fraser Lake.

Take-out: From Fraser Lake continue on Highway 16 west for 4km to the bridge crossing the Stellako River. Cross the bridge and pull out on the left. There is a small road that runs parallel to the highway and leads down to the river. This is the take-out.

Rating:
Class 2+
one Class 4 waterfall

Length: 7km

Time: 2 hours

Shuttle time: 20 minutes

Hazards:
waterfall

Put-in: The road that leads to the put-in at Francois Lake is just before the Stellako River Bridge on Highway 16, approximately 4km west of Fraser Lake. Turn left onto Francois Lake East Road and follow it for 10km. You will come to a bridge that crosses the mouth of the Stellako River at the point where it exits Francois Lake. Turn into the pullout on the right just before the bridge; this is the put-in.

Description: Immediately downstream from the put-in is a sometimes shallow, Class 2 rock garden followed by deep, slow, Class 1 water. The next kilometre contains a series of Class 2 drops where the river accelerates over boulder gardens. These drops can have large standing waves and, depending on water level, may require some manoeuvring around boulders. The river winds more with each successive drop. The next stretch is again deep, slow, Class 1 water with ideal spots for lunch, fishing and swimming.

Past this Class 1 section, the river accelerates and narrows as it approaches the waterfall. Note: power lines crossing the river are a warning that the falls are near. To prepare for the portage above the falls and to avoid the large standing waves in the middle of the river, hug the left shore. As the river bends to the right, eddy-out on the left 100m above the falls. It is also possible to eddy out on the left immediately above the falls.

The waterfall is a 5 to 6 foot drop where the river splits in two around a small island. At certain water levels advanced paddlers can run the falls. The portage is a short 25m path on river left. Below the falls the river mellows to an easy Class 1 to 2 until the take-out.
Warning: Extreme caution should be used when running the falls. There can be a dangerous keeper at the bottom of the second drop. Throw bags and rescue boats should be on hand.

Camping: Beaumont Park on Fraser Lake or Stellako Lodge on Francois Lake. Camping along the river is not permitted.

Paddling the Stellako in autumn during the salmon migration.

James Taylor

The Stellako River is lined with rock cliffs and bluffs

45 Stuart River

stuart river

At a Glance: A mostly wilderness trip on a large volume river steeped in history.

Best Time of Year: after spring flood through to fall

Maps: 93-K/8, 93-K/1, 93-J/4, 93-J/3, 93-G/13, Vanderhoof Forest District Recreation Map

Getting There: From Prince George, travel west on Highway 16 and then north on Highway 27 to Fort St. James. First, you will want to leave a vehicle at your chosen take-out location.

Put-in – Stuart Lake: On Stuart Lake or at the boat launch at the Stuart River Campground, a private campground 2km downstream on river left.

Access – Mandalay Ranch: Drive west from Vanderhoof on Highway 16 past Chilko to Sturgeon Point Road. Turn right onto Sturgeon Point Road, following this road north to the river.

Rating: Class 2+

Length:
113km on Stuart
27km on Nechako

Time: 3 days

Shuttle time: 1.5 hours

Hazards:
•sweepers
•log jams

Take-out: Take-out at Isle Pierre. To get to the Isle Pierre take-out, drive west on Highway 16 from Prince George for 35.5km to the Isle Pierre Sawmill turnoff on the right. Look for the large unique saw blade sign just after a double lane passing section returns to single lane. Follow the Isle Pierre Road for 5.5km to the sawmill. Stay left at the sawmill driving past the sawmill entrance.

Continue down the Isle Pierre Road for approximately 5km to a section where the road runs parallel to the railway. Turn at the road on the right that crosses the railway and follow this road a short distance to the old location of the Isle Pierre ferry.

Description: This large volume river is a relatively easy paddle through scenic, mostly wilderness, countryside. There are a few small rapids 2km downstream of the mouth of the river at Stuart Lake. The river then meanders slowly for 70km to near Mandalay Ranch/Creek where its velocity increases slightly. The only significant rapids on the river are the Chinlak Rapids. Watch for these 6km upstream from the Nechako River junction. These Class 2+ rapids are marked on Topographic Map 93-G/13 and consist of two sets of rapids. At higher water, expect large standing waves with some holes. In lower water, manoeuvring is required to avoid exposed rock. After the rapids, look for the grassy historic Chinlak Village site perched high on the bank on river right, 2km downstream of the rapids or 1km upstream of the Nechako River junction. There is a stairway at river level leading up to the historic site. To finish the trip, paddle down the Nechako River for 27km to Isle Pierre. To extend the trip by a day, continue on to Wilkins Park in Miworth or to Cottonwood Island Park in Prince George.

Note that approximately 66km downstream from Stuart Lake, the Sturgeon Point Road (see Access – Mandalay Ranch) meets the Stuart River. By putting in here, you can take approximately 1 day off the total trip time by skipping the slower moving upper portion of the river.

Camping: Unorganized along the river. Camping is available in Fort St. James at either a private or provincial campground.

Ken Robinson

Most of the river is a tranquil wilderness paddle.

46 Stuart Lake Provincial Parks

At a Glance: Stuart Lake has three provincial parks, Paarens Beach, Sowchea Bay and Stuart Lake Provincial Parks. This region has great historical significance and excellent fishing.

Maps: 93-K/8 (Parrens Beach and Sowchea Bay), 93-K/10 (Stuart Lake Provincial Park), Vanderhoof Forest District Recreation Map

Getting There: From Prince George, travel west on Highway 16 and then north on Highway 27 to Fort St. James. Paarens Beach and Sowchea Bay Provincial Parks are located on the south shore of Stuart Lake. Turn left on Sowchea Bay Road and drive for 15km to Paarens Beach. Sowchea Bay is located 5km further west on the road. Stuart Lake Provincial Park is located in the middle of the north shore of Stuart Lake. Drive north from Fort St. James along the North Road for approximately 6km; turn left onto the Tachie Highway just after the railway tracks. Follow this road past Pinchi and follow the signs to Stuart Lake Provincial Park.

Hazards:
- power boats
- very high winds

Description: Stuart Lake is one of the largest natural lakes in the province, approximately 70km long. It is famous for its large winds and waves so paddle with caution. Many come here to fish for its huge Lake Char and Rainbow Trout. Its shoreline is dotted with many historical sites though most are not within a reasonable paddling distance from these parks.

Camping: All three locations offer developed camping with beaches. Some sites can be reserved at Paarens Beach.

A Historical Bird's Eye View of the Stuart

With the first paddle stroke in the waters of the Stuart, the present-day paddler is invited to transcend time and join in with that special fraternity of adventurers, traders, and every-day folk who recognized and valued the life-force of this special waterway.

Long before high profile trailblazers and traders such as Fraser, Stuart, Harmon, Simpson, and Douglas plied these waters, the Stuart River had already served many centuries as the principal transportation highway for the Carrier people, or "Ta-Cuilles". Literally translated, this term means "the people who go upon the water". It is appropriate that the modern-day traveller use the canoe to visit this historically charged river, for the canoe was born and developed in the boreal forest region of North America many thousands of years ago.

The Stuart not only served as a highway, but it served as a supermarket as well. In by-gone days the many salmon runs on this waterway essentially resembled a smorgasbord on a conveyor belt. The many hundreds of food cache pits, which punctuate the banks of the entire Stuart, attest to the long-standing covenant that existed between the early inhabitants and this river system.

To begin a canoe trip on the Stuart, the present-day paddler would benefit greatly from a pre-trip tour of the reconstructed historic park in Fort St. James. The reconstruction resembles the 1890's period; however, ever since 1806 when Fraser and Stuart started the original trading post, the Stuart River served as the transportation route for resupplying the post and delivering the precious fur cargo to tide water. As early as 1815 John Stuart refers to a shipment of ninety-five packets of prime beaver pelts from this Caledonia area. Each packet contained the equivalent of sixty blanket beaver pelts and commanded a price of ten thousand pounds on the world market. The Stuart River was used as part of the major trade route until 1846 at which time alternate supply routes were established.

Much of the oral history of this region has been captured in the writings of Father Adrian G. Morice in the document The History of the Northern Interior of British Columbia. In his book Morice writes about the ancient

Indian Village of Chinlac, one of the outstanding archaeological features of the Stuart/Nechako River system. Chinlac is located on the Stuart River approximately one kilometre above its confluence with the Nechako. In 1745 a marauding band of Chilcotin Indians, to avenge the death of one of their chiefs, massacred the entire population of Chinlac Village except the chief, Khadintal, and a few others who were temporarily away from village. Morice provides vivid details of the eventual resolution of the incident in his document.

To the present-day traveller the Chinlac site appears very much as it did two and a half centuries ago. Still visible are the thirteen large rectangular lodge depressions along the top of the bank overlooking the Stuart River. Behind the two hectares prairie opening are a series of river terraces upon which in excess of two thousand food storage pits are still very evident.

For a variety of reasons Chinlac is very significant archaeologically. Size wise, the culturally modified area covers approximately 7.2km^2 in the wedged-shaped region between the Stuart and Nechako rivers. Even by world standards this is very large. The spatial arrangement of Chinlac indicates that this centrally located village was the centre of salmon harvesting and ceremonial gatherings during the proto-historic period (prior of full-fledged Western contact). Dr. Charles Borden conducted a limited excavation on Lodge #3 in the early 1950's. Within the excavated lodge approximately 1900 artifacts were located, one of which was an ancient Chinese coin that supposedly had been minted around 1125 A.D. in China. Dr. Borden did not establish the precise age of the Chinlac site; however, it appears to be totally post-Christian and it may have been occupied for about a thousand years.

Suskwa River

At a Glance: This is a short, play-filled, whitewater run in a medium volume river through some beautiful, tight canyon sections. It is a standard run for Smithers and Terrace paddlers.

Best Time of Year: usually in June or July, from 2 to 4 on the gauge.

Maps: 93-M/3, 93-M/6, Bulkley Forest District Recreation Map

Getting There: From Prince George, drive west on Highway 16 to Moricetown, 31km west of Smithers. Continue driving west approximately 36km to where the highway banks to the left up a hill. There is a gravel road turnoff on the right and a sign indicating Suskwa River Forest Road (the sign cannot be seen from the highway and the road is hard to find so look carefully). Drive downhill on the gravel road 1.5km to a bridge crossing the Bulkey River (there is a campsite on the right side). Set your odometre to zero here.

Take-out: From the bridge crossing the Bulkley River, drive 3.5km and turn left onto another gravel road. This leads approximately 1km down to a bridge crossing the Suskwa. The take-out is on river right downstream of the bridge.

Put-in: From the bridge crossing over the Bulkley River, continue on the gravel road 13km to a bridge crossing the Suskwa River. There are several choices to put in. To run the chute under the bridge, put in 50m above the bridge; to avoid the chute, put in immediately below the bridge. Alternately, cross the bridge and turn left. Drive approximately 500m to a small pull out on the left. The gauge is on river right on a rock wall at this pull out.

Rating:
(check guage at put-in)
•level below 2 - too low to paddle
•level 2 to 3.6 - Class 3
•level 3.6 to 4 - Class 3 to 3+
•level 4+ - Class 3+ to 4

Length: 11km

Time: 4 to 6 hours

Shuttle time: 15 minutes

Hazards:
•remote canyon
•must run canyon
•log jams

Description: Underneath the bridge, there is a Class 2+ to 3 chute that can easily be avoided by opting for the put-in below the bridge. From the bridge down to the river gauge, there are several Class 2 to 2+ pool-drops, followed by rock gardens requiring fast manoeuvring that lead down to the Forest Recreation Site. Below the Forest Recreation Site, the river is suitable for intermediate kayakers and advanced open boats only. Once committed on this section, there is no easy way out except downstream.

From the Forest Recreation Site, there are more Class 2 rock gardens with tight corners. The first major rapid is called The Claw. Scout on river right. The river takes a tight turn to the left then an immediate turn to the right through four rocky outcrops creating the image of a claw. The best chute is the middle one. Stay away from the log jam on river left. This rapid can be lined on river right.

After The Claw, the river narrows with tight corners and headwalls, Class 2 to 2+. The river then passes a boulder-bar on river left and turns left into the approach to the first canyon. Get out on river left and scout.

This canyon has a tricky approach with big standing waves and a chute into the canyon. Watch for logs once in the canyon. The canyon itself is Class 1+. From the first canyon, the river again has tight turns and headwalls, Class 2 to 2+.

The second large drop is called the Straight Flush, Class 3. The river turns left and flows into two chutes separated by rocky outcrops in the centre. The left chute is preferable. There is a large quiet pool at the bottom and a portage trail on the right. Scout on river right.

The approach to the second canyon is best described as a boulder bar on river right forcing the river slightly left and then a sharp right-hand turn with large diagonal waves on the outside corner. Once past this right hand turn, get out on river left and scout the canyon.

The second canyon starts with the Royal Flush, Class 3+ to 4. The river turns left and falls over a 2m ledge. There is often a clear channel in the middle and standing waves below it. Ugly keepers are on either side of this channel. This drop can be portaged on river left. The river then turns to the right through large standing waves and divides around House Rock. Take the left channel, as the right channel may be blocked with logs.

Past House Rock comes the Toilet Bowl. The river turns right and drops through a 3m gap, Class 2+. Below the Toilet Bowl, there is deep, quiet water and an old suspension bridge crossing the canyon. From there to the take-out there are a few Class 2 to 2+ drops around corners. Take out on river right below the bridge.

Camping: Just past the Bulkley River Bridge on the Suskwa Forest Service Road is a small road on the right leading down to the Bulkley River where there is unorganized camping. There is very nice camping near the put-in. From the put-in, cross the bridge and turn left. Continue on this road for approximately 1.5km passing the river gauge to a small road that leads off on the left to a forest service campsite with basic facilities.

Takla Landing to Stuart Lake

At a Glance: This system of large remote lakes and rivers takes paddlers from spectacular mountain scenery on Takla Lake, through foothills near Trembleur Lake to the interior plateau at Stuart Lake. Fishing is excellent on all lakes.

Best time of year: May to October

Maps: 93-N/3, 93-N/4, 93-N/5, 93-K/8, 93-K/9, 93-K/10, 93-K/15, Fort St. James Forest District Recreation Map.

Getting there: From Prince George, drive 100km on Highway 16 west through Vanderhoof, then turn north to Fort St. James.

Rating: Class 1 to 1+

Length:
Total distance - 190km
Takla Lake - 60km
Middle River - 40km
Trembleur Lake - 20km
Tachie River - 25km
Stuart Lake - 45km

Time: 10 days

Shuttle time: 4 hours

Hazards:
•high winds/waves
•cross lakes in early morning

Take-out: At the private Stuart River Campground located at the takeout 1.5km down the Stuart River (just south of Ft. St. James).

Put-in: Drive northeast from Fort St. James on the North Road about 4km. At the railway crossing, turn left onto the road to Tachie and Pinchi Indian Reserves. Approximately 10km past Pinchi Reserve, turn right onto the Leo Creek Forest Service Road. Drive north for 68km, then stay right on the Driftwood Forest Service Road for approximately 72km, and watch for signs to Takla Landing, where you will launch.

Description: Takla Lake is the fifth largest natural lake in the province and has much to offer in terms of scenery, fishing, and beaches. The mountain scenery is spectacular; the char and rainbow trout are large and hungry and after mid-July when water levels fall, a number of sand and gravel beaches are exposed. The west side of the lake is best for paddling and camping because a railway track runs along the east shore.

Greg Tyndall

The large mountain scenery at the northern end of Takla Lake.

Most of the Middle River, which joins Takla and Trembleur lakes, has no noticeable current and is up to a kilometre wide in places. This Provincial Heritage River has a swampy shoreline with lots of willows that provide good habitat for waterfowl. Camping spots are few and far between, but there is a nice spot by some abandoned trappers' cabins at the mouth of Van Decar Creek (about half way down the river). From there it is about three hours paddling to Trembleur Lake.

Trembleur Lake is surrounded by rolling foothills and is very beautiful. It is worth spending a few days here, so resist the temptation to travel directly across the east end of the lake to reach the Tachie River, which joins Trembleur and Stuart lakes. This 12km crossing can be very dangerous because of prevailing westerly winds. Paddle west along the shore to narrower spots that take only about half an

Greg Tyndall

Mountains give way to rolling hills towards the southern end of the lake.

hour to cross. The Tachie River is very slow moving except for a few boils and small rapids. Some manoeuvring is required to avoid rocks.

Stuart Lake is much more populated than the others, but has spectacular sandy beaches and lots of islands. Indian pictographs may be seen on the rock bluffs along the east shore of the lake between Pinchi Bay and Fort St. James. There are numerous access points where take out is possible, but the Stuart River Campground is very convenient and provides hot showers for guests!

Camping: After mid-summer when water levels decrease on the lakes, sand and gravel beaches provide great campsites. There are also a few Forestry Recreation Sites on Takla and Stuart Lakes, and the private Stuart River Campground is located at the takeout 1.5km down the Stuart River. Lodges on all three lakes provide camping and also stock food, basic supplies and, of course, beer. Camping is sparse on the Middle and Tachie Rivers. Note: much of this land is Indian Reserve and should be treated with respect and courtesy.

Telkwa River - Telkwa Forest Service Road Bridge to Old Bridge Pilings

At a Glance: This is a fun, short play run just outside of Smithers in the Village of Telkwa. It is a cold run with lots of play, especially in high water. There are few well defined eddies and some sweepers in high water, but otherwise, this is a great run for the beginner-intermediate paddler with a strong roll.

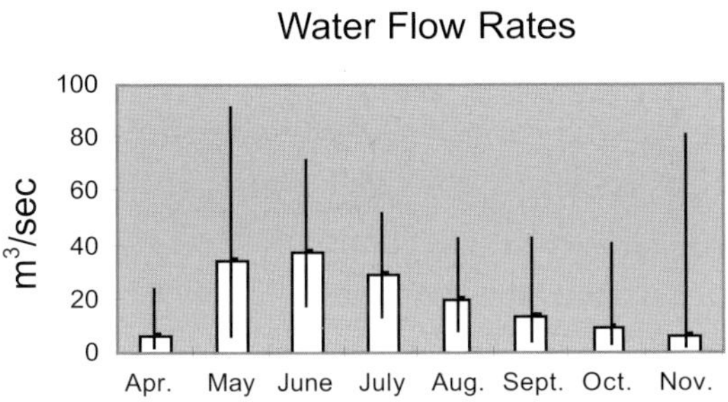

Best Time of Year: May to September. Best play is in high water, which is often in May. Flow rates taken near Tsai Creek.

Maps: 93-L/11, Bulkley Forest District Recreation Map

Rating:
- Class 2 to 2+
- Class 3 in high water

Length: 10km

Time: 2 to 3 hours

Shuttle time: 10 minutes

Hazards:
- sweepers
- log jams
- boulder garden near put-in

Getting There: From Prince George, drive west approximately 380km to the village of Telkwa. In Telkwa, turn left at the traffic lights at Hankin Street and left again onto Coalmine Road; drive another 300m to the bridge across the Bulkley River. Cross the train tracks and continue driving through a residential area. The road changes from pavement to gravel after 2km.

Take-out: After 5km on gravel, you will pass the hydro plant on the right, and shortly after that, Goathorn Creek Bridge. Stay to the right after crossing the bridge. At km 0 on the Telkwa River Forest Service Road, turn to the right; the take-out is 700m down this road. There is ample parking here but no camping.

Put-in: Return to the main road and drive another 5km to where the road crosses the Telkwa River. Cross the bridge and put in on the right side. There is a campsite on river left, across the bridge. There is ample parking here, picnic tables and outhouses.

Description: Just above the bridge is a fantastic surf wave, which is a great warm-up for the run. Heading downstream is a long stretch (2km) of flat water, which has a lot of one-timer holes at high water and gets quite shallow at low water; stay to river left of the middle at low water. The river turns to the right and enters a short boulder garden. At the base of the approaching headwall is a large friendly eddy where you'll have time to adjust your outfitting and undo a friend's drain-plug. Immediately beside the eddy is the 'ender corner', which, as the name suggests, is an excellent venue for practicing some of kayaking's more 'dated' manoeuvres. Watch for large log jams along the river right bank here.

Have a rest as you drift through two more wide meanders. On the outside left corner of a right hand bend is The Terminator. This is a huge hole with some sticky play that should be scouted before dropping in. Run right-of-centre and scout the hole from the eddy below. Carry on to the run's best surf, creatively named 'The Wave Train.' The best eddy is on the right. Flat spin as the sun sets in front of you. Blow off the front wave and throw some ends through the rest of the train. At higher water levels it is worth hiking up the gravel bar to catch a river-wide wave above the wave train.

Approximately the last 3km have some more waves, ledges and holes that can easily be avoided. A short canyon creates a powerful eddy on the right. Peel-in, rescue a swimmer and stern squirt as you peel-out. Smile as you paddle through another 1km of Class 2+ boulder gardens and wave trains. Below is the Telkwa's last chance wave (unnamed), a one-timer on the left. Be mindful of sweepers. Look for the take-out some 200m below on the right by some old bridge pilings.

NOTE 1: There is good road access to the river above the put-in bridge, but generally the river consists of too many log jams and a lot of flat water. The section 1km above the put-in bridge is boulder-strewn and fun.

NOTE 2: From the old bridge pilings, you can paddle down to where the Telkwa River meets the Bulkley River, a distance of approximately 5 - 7km. The take-out is at Eddy Park on Howson Avenue, right by the local Telkwa pub. This section has two Class 2+ drops. Again, this section is loaded with log jams, some sections are quite braided with shallows. At certain water levels, there is some surfing at the confluence of the Bulkey and the Telkwa Rivers.

Camping: Organized camping is available at Thyee Lake Provincial Park in Telkwa. Unorganized at the put-in.

James Taylor

Play safe! Practice getting over obstacles in the river.

50

ten mile lake

Ten-Mile Lake Provincial Park

At a Glance: A popular destination to dip your paddle near the City of Quesnel.

Maps: 93-G/1, Cariboo Forest Region Recreation Map (East)

Getting There: The park is located 12km north of Quesnel on Highway 97. From Prince George, drive south on Highway 97 to the town of Hixon. From here continue south on Highway 97 for 41.5km to the bridge over the Cottonwood River. Continue 5km south to the park.

Length: 6km

Hazards: powerboats

Description: Great fishing in the spring is the main draw for paddlers. In summer, the three beaches and warm water make this a great place to practice boating skills.

Camping: Full facility camping is available.

Jim Card

Prince George paddling club volunteers work to keep an access trail in good shape.

Torpy River

The Torpy River offers two very different trips. For canoe tripping enjoy a 3-day trip on the lower section down to the Fraser River. Camping is mostly on sand/gravel bars and wildlife sightings can be frequent. A first descent of another canyoned stretch of the river was recently made, unveiling an exciting day trip for the advanced whitewater boater. Run numerous 1 to 3 metre drops and have a look at the two 10 metre falls enroute.

Sean Fraser

The second set of falls on the Torpy River.

Torpy River - Middle Canyon

At a Glance: This section of the river is small volume through narrow, steeply walled canyons. The run contains lots of action for the advanced paddler with numerous 1 to 3 metre drops as well as two 10-metre waterfalls. Rope and rappel equipment is required to portage around the waterfalls.

Best Time of Year: At medium water levels after snowmelt or rainfall. This run has not been done at higher water levels.

Maps: 93-I/3, Prince George Forest District Recreation Map

Getting There: Starting at the Yellowhead Bridge in Prince George, drive east on Highway 16 for 14.5km to the turnoff for the Upper Fraser Road. Turn left onto the Upper Fraser Road. Follow this road past the town of Upper Fraser and cross the Fraser River on the Hansard Railway Bridge. All roads are gravel after this bridge. This drive takes approximately 1 hour.

Rating:
Class 4+
2 Class 5 waterfalls

Length: 3km

Time: 4 hours

Shuttle time: 15 minutes

Hazards:
•log jams
•sweepers
•waterfalls are difficult to portage
•2nd falls requires rappel kit and ropes to lower boats

Continue for approximately 1km to the old McGregor Camp location and turn left onto the Pass Lake Forest Service Road. Continue on the Pass Lake Road for 30km, and turn right onto the Lower Torpy Road. Drive for 2km on the Lower Torpy Road and turn left onto the Upper Torpy Road.

Take-out: The take-out is at kilometre 2.1 on the Upper Torpy Road. Just before the road begins to climb a hill, hike down a rough trail on the right to the river and mark the take-out location.

Put-in: Continue along the Upper Torpy Road to kilometre 5.2. There is a small pull-out on the right and a trail leads down to the river through old logging to an obvious large cottonwood tree at the rivers edge.

Description: This section of the Torpy River is small volume through narrow canyons, and as such, water levels are very dependant on rainfall and snowmelt. The river is shallow with many rock gardens and contains numerous small drops of 1 to 3m. The run starts with a Class 2 boulder garden. Watch and listen for the first major waterfall approximately 800m from the put-in, which occurs on a blind corner. Pull-out on river right to portage. Though this 10 metre fall has been run once, the line is very difficult and portaging is recommended.

Continue in the steep walled canyon running several 1 to 3m drops, Class 4 to 4+, down to the second set of falls. These falls are approximately 300m from the first set and are again about 10m high. Run the falls or portage on left. You will need to lower your boat on rope as well as rappel yourself down to the river as the canyon at this point is very steeply walled.

After the second set of falls the river continues with some 1 to 3m drops and boulder gardens down to the take-out, Class 3 to 4.

Hardy Griesbauer

Preparing to run a drop.

Camping: At the forest recreation campsite at Pass Lake (kilometer 38 of the Pass Lake Road) or any of the other nearby forest recreation site.

Torpy River - West Torpy Bridge to Dome Creek

At a Glance: This medium volume river meanders throughout and offers nice views of the surrounding McGregor Mountains and frequent wildlife sightings. There is a great deal of active logging in the area, but this shouldn't stop paddlers from enjoying this pleasant tripping river.

Best Time of Year: June or July during medium water levels.

Maps: 93-I/3, 93-H/14, 93-H/15, 93-H/10, Prince George Forest District Recreation Map

Rating: Class 1 to 2

Length: 96km

Time: 3 days

Shuttle time: 2 to 3 hours

Hazards:
- log jams
- sweepers

Getting There: Starting at the Yellowhead Bridge in Prince George, drive east on Highway 16 for 14.5km to the turnoff for the Upper Fraser Road.

Put-in: Turn left onto the Upper Fraser Road. Follow this road past the town of Upper Fraser and cross the Fraser River on the Hansard Railway Bridge. All roads are gravel after this bridge. This drive takes approximately 1 hour. Continue for approximately 1km to the old McGregor Camp location and turn left onto the Pass Lake Forest Service Road.

Continue on the Pass Lake Road for 30km, and turn right onto the Torpy Road. Drive for 5km on the Torpy Road to the bridge crossing the Torpy River, the put-in. Do not worry about the small volume of water as the main river joins 200m downstream. The Torpy Road continues part of the way downstream on the right side.

Take-out: From the junction of Highway 16 and the Upper Fraser Road, drive east on Highway 16 approximately 100km to the Dome Creek turnoff. Turn left down this road and continue 8km to the community of Dome Creek. There is no road access to the mouth of the Torpy River, so paddlers must take out on the Fraser River, either at Dome Creek 16km below the Torpy where the railway crosses the Fraser River, or at one of the private landings about 8km upstream from Dome Creek, if permission is received from the owners. When shuttling vehicles, use the Bowron Forest Service Road that crosses Highway 16 east of Purden Lake and runs 27km north to near the old McGregor Camp (see the forest service recreation map).

Description: The top third of the river is mostly gravel bottom and very shallow in places. The next third is very slow with clay and peat banks. There are some rock gardens and fast water between the halfway cabin and Walker Creek that could become Class 2 at higher water levels. Because of the narrow channels and many sweepers and log jams, the ability to back-ferry is essential, especially in the upper part. The river drops about 125m from the put-in to the mouth.

Camping: Unorganized along the river. There is an excellent spot just across the bridge at the put-in; otherwise, gravel bars with log jams on the upper third of the river provide suitable campsites. There are very few campsites through the area of clay banks until the guide cabin is reached, about halfway down the run. There are several good spots between the cabin and Walker Creek.

52 tudyah lake

Tudyah Lake Provincial Park

At a Glance: Located near the City of Mackenzie, this park offers fishing and wildlife viewing opportunities.

Maps: 93-O/3, Prince George Forest District Recreation Map

Getting There: From Prince George drive north on Highway 97 to the town of McLeod Lake. The park is a further 9km.

Length: 8km

Hazards:
- high winds
- power boats

Description: Explore the narrow river channels of the Pack River, which flows through the lake on its way to Williston Lake. The lakes interesting shoreline also provides the paddler the opportunity to find a secluded bay to relax and fish in.

Camping: A variety of campsites are available on a first come first serve basis. Enjoy the beach available to campers.

Marian Tamkin

World Class paddlers like Lyle Dickieson cut their teeth on the club gates on the Lower Willow River.

Wansa Creek Culvert

At a Glance: This is a true park and play spot beside the highway. Paddlers can run through a culvert that drops into a deep pool with good eddy access. Practice your cartwheels or stern squirts in the outflow until you drop from exhaustion.

Best Time of Year: in warmer water as you will be rolling a lot.

Maps: 93-G/16, Prince George Forest District Recreation Map

Getting There: From Prince George, drive 32km east on Highway 16 from the Yellowhead Bridge to the Willow River Bridge. Note your odometre here. Continue another 5km to the Wansa Creek Culvert. Make sure you park well off to the side of the highway.

Description: The Wansa Creek Culvert flows under Highway 16 and is large enough to paddle through. The culvert drops 1 to 3 feet, depending on water levels, into a pool. The outflow of the culvert is good for practicing cartwheels or stern squirts in kayaks. Since you will be upside down a lot, it is also a good location to practice your roll in turbulent water. Wansa Creek itself is not large enough to paddle.

Rating: Class 2

Hazards:
•debris in culvert
•sweepers downstream
•bolts and fish baffles
•boat could wedge in culvert

Camping: Good camping is available at the Willow River Forest Recreation Site, known locally as the 'Gravel Pit'. To get to the 'Gravel Pit' proceed 1.1km past the Willow River Bridge on Highway 16 and turn right onto a gravel road. Approximately 200m down this road from the highway, you will come to a fork in the road. Take the fork to the right to reach the forest recreation site.

54 West Lake

west lake

At a Glance: West Lake is typical of lakes in the Prince George area. It is surrounded by rolling hills covered with evergreen and deciduous trees. This lake is one of the closest to Prince George, so it makes a good destination for a quick paddle or roll practice session. A large public beach and picnic area is located on the north end of the lake.

Best time of year: May to October

Maps: 93-G/10, Prince George Forest District Recreation Map

Length: 5km

Hazards:
•occasional strong winds

Getting There: From Prince George drive 10km west on Highway 16 and turn left onto Blackwater Road. In approximately 12km turn left onto West Lake Road. In a few kilometres you will see signs directing you either to the boat launch or the public beach.

Description: West Lake is fairly populated with summer cottages and a few year-round homes, so it can be very busy with boat traffic in July and August. The south end of the lake has no development and supports a few large families of geese, so it is worthwhile paddling to this end. In autumn, traffic on the lake seems to disappear. On crisp, bright, autumn days, after the leaves have turned yellow, paddling is prime.

Camping: Camping is only possible at the south end of the lake, but it is not recommended as it might disturb the geese.

Marian Tamkin

A great place to practice paddling skills of all sorts.

55 whiskers point

Whiskers Point Provincial Park (McLeod Lake)

At a Glance: A nice family destination for swimming and boating.

Maps: 93-J/15, Prince George Forest District Recreation Map

Getting There: From Prince George drive north to McLeod Lake (38km north of the town Bear Lake).

Description: This park is situated on a sandy point jutting into McLeod Lake. Enjoy the sandy beach and explore the lakes shoreline and the Crooked River flowing into the lake at its southern end.

Camping: There are many lakeside, forested campsites to choose-from in the park.

Length: 20km

Hazards:
- high winds
- power boats

Ken Robinson

At Whiskers Point you can enjoy a sandy beach much like this one on Tsacha Lake.

Willow River

This small volume river flows mostly through evergreen and deciduous forests, passing through occasional sand cut-banks and one impressive rock canyon. Even though the surrounding area has been extensively logged, the Willow maintains a wilderness feel. It features Class 1 to Class 4+ water, as well as an impassable canyon just downstream of the Highway 16 Bridge. There are a number of access points to the river, so trips from a few hours to 3 days can be planned.

Three very popular whitewater sections offer challenges for novices (The Upper), intermediates (The Lower) and advanced paddlers (The Lower Lower). Detailed descriptions of these trips are described in separate reports. Good day trips for canoeists might include a run from Buckhorn or Pitoney Bridge to the Forest Service Recreation Site. Or, if you have time for a longer shuttle, the trip from Stony Lake Bridge to Pitoney Bridge is recommended. Day trips for canoeists are also possible from the Lower Lower take-out to the Beaver Forest Road Bridge (a long day), or from the Beaver Forest Bridge to Willow River town site, or Shelley.

Marian Tamkin

Rescue time, a frequent scene below Freak-My-Beak.

Stony Lake Bridge to Forest Service Recreational Site

At a Glance: This section is suitable for canoe tripping. The river runs through evergreen forests, and in lower water levels, many gravel bars provide opportunities to camp and swim. Features such as tight turns, rocks, waves, head-walls, sweepers and log jams are guaranteed to keep paddlers alert. Day trips from a few hours to a full day are possible depending on put-ins and take-outs. Novice kayakers who enjoy the Upper Willow may also enjoy the segment between Pitoney and Buckhorn bridges, or the longer section from Buckhorn Bridge to the BC Forest Recreation Site. This section should not be run in high water because of log jams.

Best Time of Year: summer or fall when water levels are lower. Water levels can be checked on the gauge under the Willow River Bridge on Highway 16. Levels above 3.0 are considered high for this trip.

Rating: Class 2

Length:
Stony Lake B. to Pitoney B. - 36km
Pitoney B. to Buckhorn B. - 10km
Buckhorn B. to Rec. Site - 19km

Time:
Stony Lake B. to Pitoney B. - 6 hours
Pitoney B. to Buckhorn B. - 2 hours
Buckhorn B. to Rec. Site - 4 hours

Shuttle time:
total trip - 1.5 hours
consecutive put-ins - 0.5 hours

Maps: 93-H/5, 93-H/12, 93-G/9, 93-G/16, Prince George Forest District Recreation Map.

Getting there: Starting at the Yellowhead Bridge, drive 32km on Highway 16 east to the Willow River Bridge. Approximately 1km past the bridge turn right onto Willow-North Forestry Road (no signs).

Take-out: From the intersection with Highway 16, drive approximately 200m to a fork in the road. Take the road on the right and drive1km to the Forest Service Recreation Site on the bank of the Willow River.

Access Locations: There are three good access locations upstream, all where bridges cross the river.

Access #2 – Buckhorn Bridge: From the intersection with Highway 16 (see above), drive approximately 200m to the fork in the road. Take the left road and drive 19km until you reach Buckhorn Bridge. This bridge can also be reached from Highway 97 south by turning left onto the Willow Forest Service Road, approximately 16km south of the intersection of Highways 97 and 16. Follow this road for 9km to a T-junction; turn right and you will reach Buckhorn Bridge in approximately 20km.

Access #1 – Pitoney Bridge: If you have arrived at the Buckhorn Bridge from Highway 16, cross the bridge and turn left. Pitoney Bridge is a further 10km. If you have arrived from Highway 97, veer right just before Buckhorn Bridge and follow the road 10km to Pitoney Bridge.

Put-in – Stony Lake Bridge: Cross Pitoney Bridge and drive 37km to the Stony Lake Bridge, staying right at the two major intersections on the way. There are two more bridges upstream of Stony Lake Bridge, but word has it that if you put in at these, you will be pulling your canoe over many beaver dams that block this slow, meandering section.

Description: The entire stretch from Stony Lake Bridge to the Forest Service Recreational Site is quite scenic with evergreen forests bordering the river banks most of the way. Downstream of Stony Lake Bridge, the Willow is Class 1 containing some boulders and riffles. The boulders are easy to avoid, but occasionally you might bottom-out in a riffle and have to get out to drag your boat.

From Narrow Creek to the Forest Service Recreational Site, the Willow is Class 1 to 2 at summer water levels. Some Class 2 sections contain standing waves and boulders that are hard to see until you are very close to them. Log jams are common. Approximately 5km below Pitoney Bridge, there is a short canyon with a left turn. Rocks just below the canyon provide good eddies at lower water. At high water, most of these rocks are flooded over and there is considerable turbulence and a few log jams.

For several kilometers below Buckhorn Bridge there are many rocks to catch on the fly. These rocks and surf waves, however, are easy to avoid. After this section, the water becomes Class 1 as the river wends its way around many islands. Scout carefully from your boat because log jams are common and can span the river. Approximately 10km below Buckhorn Bridge darkly colored cut banks mark a sharp bend to the right. Most of the water piles against high banks on river left and then forms standing waves. There is an old mine on river left to explore. The last 5km of this section is known as the Upper Willow and is described in a separate section. Don't miss the take-out at the Forestry Service Recreational Site on river right because there is a canyon below this that is only suitable for advanced paddlers at favorable water levels.

Ed Day

Practicing rodeo moves, this is the main play spot of the otherwise novice run

Camping: The first good campsite below Stony Lake Bridge is at Narrow Creek at an old sawmill site. Another campsite, at Buckhorn Bridge, is a deactivated Forest Service site so has flat tent spots but no outhouse. The best campsite is at the Forest Service Recreation site at the take-out and features picnic tables and an outhouse. In the summer when water levels are down, sand and gravel bars provide plenty of camping.

Willow River – Upper

At a Glance: This is one of the favourite runs close to the town of Prince George. The river is a good novice run but also can have a great play hole for more advanced paddlers.

Best Time of Year: Check the river gauge under the Willow River Bridge on Highway 16. The gauge can be viewed from the bridge on the river left upstream side. The play spot is good when the level is 5 or greater on the gauge. The run is good year-round as a novice run though at higher water levels, it is pushier.

Maps: 93-G/16, Prince George Forest District Recreation Map

Getting There: From Prince George, drive 32km east on Highway 16 from the Yellowhead Bridge to the Willow River Bridge. Proceed 1.1km past the bridge to a small turn off on the right. Take this turn off.

Rating: Class 2

Length: 3km

Time: 1 hour

Shuttle time: 5 minutes

Hazards:
- log jams
- sweepers

Take-out: Approximately 200m from the highway turn-off, you will come to a fork in the road. Take the fork to the right to the forest recreation site, known locally as the 'Gravel Pit', and the take-out.

Put-in: Approximately 200m from the highway turn-off, you will come to a fork in the road. Take the fork to the left. Approximately 2km further down this road, you will come to a second fork in the road with a short pull-out on the right. Take the pull-out on the right and park here for the put-in.

Description: This section of the river is ideal for an evening paddle for beginners and intermediates wanting to brush up on their paddling skills. To start, stay on the left side of the channel to avoid the log jam on the outside of the first left turn. The river then opens up to a gentle Class 1 to 2. The river is dotted with rocks and riverside eddies. However, at high water (above 2) many eddies are washed out or are crowded with tree branches. For more advanced paddlers, there is an excellent play hole on river left approximately 500m downstream of the put-in. This is the best hole in the Prince George area and local paddlers use it frequently to tune their rodeo skills.

Camping: The forest recreation site at the take-out is a beautiful spot by the river that is frequented by hunters, tree planters, fishers, campers and paddlers.

The Big Chill

Early morning fog shrouds the street lights. The pavement is slick with black ice. Darkness lingers through breakfast. Paddling season is finally over. Or is it?

Peeling back layers of sleep, five fools fill thermoses with boiling liquids. By the time they meet, the morning is icy grey. The five each wonder to themselves, "Why?"

Arriving at the river, they begin the fastest shuttle and change on record. Its so cold the flush mechanism in the outhouse is frozen. So are Steve's airbags. There is a dusting of snow to the river's edge. Ribald humour masks the apprehensive shivering. Eventually, the five kayaks drift down the river. Icicles dangle along the banks. Mist starts to rise with the sound of more ribald humour. Just above the first drop, for no good reason, Steve flips. Lots of screaming. Ice Cream Headache #1.

Surfing is good. And careful! No more flips. Rick decides to backsurf. He flips. Ice Cream Headache #2.

"I'm getting cold you guys. Let's roll."
"No way man!"
Playing is good. Muscles are finally loose and warm. At least it feels that way. Maybe the brain's frozen.
Rushhhhhh through the canyon. Out they go, surviving another run on the Willow.

Pouring tea and feeling fine at the take-out, they check for missing gonads. "An icy river, mildewed wetsuits, frozen fingers, and friends shuttling in from all over. I tell you Ian, these are the best of times!

Willow River – Lower

At a Glance: This is the town of Prince George's staple run. This run is relatively close to town, provides excitement at many water levels for intermediate and advanced paddlers, and is the location of the club's Paddlefest held annually in June.

Best Time of Year: Check the river gauge under the Willow River Bridge on Highway 16 and scout for logs. The gauge can be viewed from the bridge on the river left upstream side. Play is best between –1.0 and +2.0 on the gauge. Between +2.0 and +4.0 on the gauge, most play spots become washed out. Above +4.0 on the gauge, the river becomes quite pushy and a large keeper forms below house rock at about +5.0. The river is not recommended above +4.0. The river can be run safely below 1+ on the guage.

Maps: 93-G/16, Prince George Forest District Recreation Map

Rating:
(check gauge at Hwy 16 bridge)
level below 0 - Class 2+
level 0 to 4.5 - Class 3
level 5 - Class 3+
level 6 to 7.5 - Class 4 to 5
level 8 to 9 - Class 4

Length: 2km

Time: 30 minutes

Shuttle Time: 5 minutes

Hazards:
- log jams
- impassable canyon below take-out
- logs in canyon after high water (can scout canyon from trail on east side of river)

Getting There: From Prince George, drive 32km east on Highway 16 from the Yellowhead Bridge to the Willow River Bridge. Stop and read the gauge (see above).

Take-out: Just before the Willow River Bridge, there is a short road on the left that leads to a rest stop. Park at the rest stop, making sure you leave room for RV's and 5th wheel trailers to turn around.

Put-in: Proceed 1.1km past the bridge to a small turn off on the right. Take this turn off. Approximately 200m from the highway turn-off, you will come to a fork in the road. Take the fork to the right to the forest recreation site, known locally as the 'Gravel Pit', and the put-in.
Description: Class 2 water below the

put-in allows some time to warm up for the more technical water to follow. Where the canyon walls start, the aptly named First Drop rapid signals the start of the canyon. There is a large eddy on river right below First Drop as well as smaller eddies on river left.

Below First Drop, there is a short boulder garden and then a short rapid bending to the right that ends in a large pool. Stay to the left through this section as logs often plug a small channel on the right. Below the pool, the river splits at Log Rock. Again, take the left channel as the right channel often is blocked with logs. Just below Log Rock is Diamond Wave. This wave/hole is prime for 360's and flat spins around –1.0 on the gauge.

Wayne Giles

Surf City, a favourite spot where locals can spend hours.

Just below Diamond Wave, a small creek enters on river left in the middle of a turbulent wave-filled section. At the bottom of this section, another large rock is in the centre of the river. Shortly after this, there is a near river-wide wave/hole named Surf City. The eddies are well placed hereand enable you to have numerous tries at the wave/hole. Between –1.0 and +0.5, the wave is more of a hole with good side surfing, spinning and cartwheeling opportunities.

The hole becomes a prime surf wave at about +1.5 on the gauge. Surf City is an optional take-out location if you do not want to run 'Freak-My-Beak', the most difficult drop on the run. This 3 to 4 foot drop is usually run by approaching from just right of centre moving to the left aiming to go over the drop 2 to 3 feet off the rock on river left. At some water levels, the river tends to pile into the cliff walls below the drop on river left.

Once through Freak-My-Beak, either upside down or right-side-up, make sure you keep your boat pointing straight downstream on river left to run the channel on the left of House Rock. House Rock has eaten many canoes and kayaks over the years. House Rock develops into an ugly keeper when the gauge is 5 to 7.5 and it is not recommended to run the canyon at these levels. Below House Rock, there are a few more play waves as the river bends to the right at Last

Marian Tamkin

Freak my Beak!

Drop. Once past Last Drop, it is easy Class 1 to the take-out, 250m downstream on river left by a small sandy beach.
WARNING: There is an impassable canyon below the take-out that took the lives of eight unsuspecting teenagers in the mid-1970's

Camping: At the forest recreation site at the put-in. This locale known as the 'Gravel Pit' is a beautiful spot by the river that is frequented by hunters, tree planters, fishers, campers and paddlers. This is the location of the annual Prince George Paddlefest.

The Lower Lower: Life From Death

There had been a long period when nobody thought to run the section of river below the Killer Canyon. The reason for this was the tragic deaths of eight young men in 1974, that were going to go for a tranquil float down the apparently benign Willow River. Unfortunately, their trip ended soon in the hungry jaws of what is now termed the Killer Canyon. That stretch of river is truly wild and has never been paddled. A monument to these young kids stands in the Willow River rest stop.

In June of 1993, a few people who walked up river during very low water from the take-out scouted the Lower Lower section. The rumour was that it could be run. So in early June of that year, when many of the regular runs had become a bit boring and the river was running at about 2 on the gauge, Bart Wagner and Ed Day decided they were going to run it. After some trepidation, they decided to go for it. These two had a mission! Things went pretty well all the way. They spent considerable time scouting and had a successful run. Ed lost his sunglasses as a token to the River Gods at Gambler's Choice and he smashed and broke the bottom of his glass Cruise Control again, in the very last drop of the run. This was the second time in two weeks. Anyway, after that 'all clear' run, this section has become a bread and butter run for the locals throughout the summer and fall. It is truly a wonderful place for which we are all thankful.

Willow River – Lower Lower

At a Glance: Although this run is short, it is action packed. Expect many drops and plenty of holes for play and practicing the latest moves on this narrow, twisting, canyoned river. There are great stretches that are fun for squirting, rock splatting, and working on technical eddy hopping.

Best Time of Year: Check the river gauge under the Willow River Bridge on Highway 16. The gauge can be viewed from the bridge on the river left upstream side. Best levels are below 2 on the gauge. Ideal play conditions are between 3/4 to 1 3/4. Levels above 2 on the gauge get very pushy. This run is not recommended above 3 1/2 on the gauge.

Maps: 93-G/16, Prince George Forest District Recreation Map

Rating:
•gauge 2 to 3.5 - Class 4
•gauge less than 2 - Class 4-

Length: 4km

Time: 1 hour

Shuttle time: 5 minutes

Hazards:
•log jams
•dangerous put-in trail

Getting There: From the Highway 16 Bridge over the Fraser River in Prince George, drive east 32km to the Willow River Bridge and read the gauge. 1km before you reach the bridge, there is a Demonstration Forest access road on the north side of the road (left side when driving east). Take this gravel road for about 2km until you see a small parking lot on the right side of the road. This lot is for the Killer Canyon viewpoint.

Put-in: Drive 50m further down the road to the trail down to the Lower Lower. A flagged trail goes steeply down hill. Be advised to tether your boat when you get to the really steep part. Avoid going down the trail after a rain-storm. It could be fatal for you or your companions as this is a very rough put-in trail.

Take-out: Continue down the road for 2 to 3km. You will see a small cart track on your right. Park here. From the river, you can find the take-out by looking for a large rock in the middle of the river, approximately 1km downstream from the last play spot. 200m beyond this, watch for flagging tape on the left shore and a steep, well-worn, trail heading straight up an embankment. Allow about 15 minutes to get to the top of the trail.

Description: Once on the water, there is a nice twisty section of about 100 metres of easy paddling before the first drop. The first drop, Royal Flush, flows out of a slow moving pool. Although this is often scouted from river right, it is possible to scout it from a small eddy on the left just above the drop. The drop has been safely run pretty well everywhere both forwards and backwards. Many paddlers like the left side because there is a rockslide move and it lines you up best to punch the small hole on the bottom. There is a catchment eddy on the right at the end of the drop, but be prepared to paddle hard for it or you will be into the next section, which starts immediately.

Chad Ridsdale

The Royal Flush

When you look downstream, there is a large rock that sticks above the water on the left about 25 metres downstream of the last drop. Most often, this section is run to the left of the rock through an S-turn drop. However, it is navigable on the right side as well, but you have to punch through the middle of the holes rather than the edges. The section continues with many eddies to catch, mainly on the left. Here you are halfway down the rapid.

Looking downstream of the S-turn drop, you will again see a large rock in the middle of the channel. That rock indicates the end of the rapid; call it Gambler's Choice. Before you get there, go extreme left for an easy ledge drop and a good line for the Choice, or go right down a convoluted passage laced with holes. Just above Gambler's Choice, you can either go center-left and do a rock slide/boof move trying to miss the meat of the deep hole at the bottom, or do a fancy ferry right above the rock and go right into another deep, sticky hole. Frequently, paddlers choose the left and end up in the hole on the right anyway. There is a nice pool to collect the pieces just past the holes.

During one paddler's first run down this section, his Carrera sunglasses held on by Croakies under his helmet were ripped off his head as he dropped into the left hole straight on, disappeared and resurfaced downstream in an explosive rocket move. It was spectacular but costly! This season he swam out of the right hole after getting typewritered in from the left. For the remainder of the season, he decided to go right and dig his way out straight on rather than chance a sideways encounter.

Next, the section starts out playfully with a bunch of easy eddies, then it gets narrower and steeper. Soon you will see the water drop into a 5 metre wide slot. This is the beginning of Crap Shoot, so eddy out on river left above the shoot to scout the downstream section. Look for logs in the tight passages around the rocks. There is usually a strong left to right diagonal curler here that flips a lot of boaters. If you flip, roll up fast because you have to move left to complete the shoot. A large rock constricts the passage called, Hit Me, and it is turbulent and unpredictable going through. Another nice eddy awaits you below this.

Below here the river sluices back and forth for about 50 metres to another large eddy on the right. There is a good little ender / cartwheel spot there, but watch for some subsurface boulders residing just down from the spot. From here, the end of the fun section is visible.

The next little drop is Roulette. Eddy out behind the midstream rock and try out one of the best ender spots around. If you try cartwheels here, you will soon be spinning like a roulette wheel! This is one of the main reasons paddlers come here. They will paddle down to here in 20 to 30 minutes and then spend several hours here getting flipped continuously. Downstream, it is about 1.2km to the take-out. There are a few modestly entertaining features along the way.

Camping: At the well-developed forest recreation site at the put-in. This locale known as thc 'Gravel Pit' is a beautiful spot by the river that is frequented by hunters, tree planters, fishers, campers and paddlers. This is the location of the annual Prince George Paddlefest

Trail Classifications

Local paddlers like to rate put-in trails as well as the rivers. In the case of the Lower Lower, this river has a class 5 put-in trail, one of the highest rated in the region. Once during a rodeo event here one of the competitors dropped his boat. Even though it was tethered, the tether broke and down went the boat. Fortunately, he wanted to be the first down the trail and nobody was below him. Needless to say, the boat got to the bottom, skimmed across the water and started downstream by itself. Since you cannot walk the shoreline in this steep sided canyon, the young man ran back up the trail and down the road to the take-out, incredibly, without any shoes on! Eventually he did retrieve his boat at the end of the canyon, about 500m upstream of the take-out. You might say that in this case, haste makes waste because he did not get a run in that afternoon. Be careful on this trail!

Willow River - Lower Lower take-out to Fraser River

At a Glance: The put-in for this section is towards the bottom of a narrow canyon, and although the water is Class 1 from here, the valley is fairly narrow and features rocky banks. Below Wansa Creek, the valley widens and paddlers can view forested hills in the distance and cottonwood stands along the river. Many log jams require either portaging or careful manoeuvring.

Best Time of Year: summer and fall when water levels are lower

Maps: 93-G/1, 93-G/16, 93-J/1, 93-J/2, Prince George Forest District Recreation Map

Rating: Class 1+

Length:
Lower Lower take-out to Beaver Forest Rd. - 25km
Beaver Forest Rd. to Willow River townsite - 12km
Willow River townsite to Shelley - 18km

Time:
Lower-Lower take-out to Beaver Forest Rd - 9 hours
Beaver Forest Road to Willow R town site: 3 hours
Willow R town site to Shelley: 4 hours

Shuttle time: 3/4 hour or less between access points

Hazards:
•log jams
•log jams are dangerous in high water

Getting there: Access to the put-in and to the take-out are on different roads, both accessible from Highway 16 east. To reach the put-in, turn left onto the Demonstration Forest access road, 31km from Yellowhead Bridge (1km before the Highway 16 bridge across the Willow River). The take-out is at Shelley, so turn left onto Shelley road 9km from Yellowhead Bridge over the Fraser River.

Put-in: Take the Demonstration Forest access road for about 2km until you see a small parking lot on the right side of the road. From this parking lot, you can walk a short trail to view an impassable canyon. Continue past this parking lot for 2 to 3km until you see a small cart track on your right. Park here and follow a trail down to the river. Be very careful to put-in at the correct place because just upstream of this is the section known as the Lower Lower, and it is rated as Class 4.

Access #1 – Beaver Road: From Shelley, continue on the Beaver Forest Road until kilometre 26 where the road crosses the Willow River.

Access #2 – Willow River Town Site: From Shelley, continue on the Beaver Forest Road until approximately kilometre 18, then turn left onto Upper Fraser Road. A bridge crosses the river at Willow River town site 7km from this intersection.

Take-out: From the intersection of Shelley Road and Highway 16, drive approximately 12km to Shelley. There is a boat launch and parking area immediately downstream of the sawmill.

Description: Between the put-in and Wansa Creek, the river is fairly swift. There are few if any log jams in this section. After Wansa Creek, the Willow River flows through a wide, attractive valley of broad leaf and evergreen forests, and closer to the river there are many beautiful cottonwood stands. Log jams are common, and canoeists must be skilled enough to manoeuvre through these. Some log jams span the width of the river and portaging is necessary. The river is mostly Class 1; however, the log jams would make this a dangerous run in high water. There is a short Class 3 rapid that begins just above the Beaver Forest Road Bridge and continues under the bridge. Scout this rapid and portage if necessary. The Fraser River is big, but it is easy Class 1. There may be a few strong eddy lines and boils. On this trip you might see moose, bear, beaver and a variety of birds.

Camping: Camping is possible on the many sand and gravel bars throughout this section in lower water levels.

Trip Grouping Index

This index groups trips according to their type, difficulty, and length.

Extended Lake Trips: offer multi-day canoe tripping on remote lakes.

Lake Day Trips: short day excursions to lakes, great for family outings

Multi-Day River Trips: moving water trips from Novice up to Class 2

6	Bowron River
16	Crooked River
22	Fraser River - Tete Jaune to Quesnel
26	McGregor River – Herrick Creek to Fraser River
27	Morice River
29	Murray River
35	Nechako River
36	Pack River
37	Parsnip River
38	Pine River - East Pine to Taylor
42	Raush River
43	Salmon River - 600 Road to Fraser River (Shelley)
45	Stuart River
51	Torpy River (West Torpy Bridge to Dome Creek)
56	Willow River - Stony Lake Bridge to Forest Service

Advanced / Intermediate Whitewater Day Trips: plenty of action up to class 3

4	Blackwater River – Batnuni Bridge to Blackwater Bridge and Blackwater Bridge to Fraser River
6	Bowron River - Portage Canyon to Lyle's Lawn
25	Horsefly River - The Steps to Recreation Site
35	Nechako River - Isle Pierre and Whitemud Rapids
41	Quesnel River - Lower
44	Stellako River
49	Telkwa River - Telkwa Forest Service Road Bridge to Old Bridge Pilings
56	Willow River - Lower

Advanced Whitewater Day Trips: great whitewater for the adrenaline junkie

2	Baker Creek
7	Canoe River - Water Gauge to Highway 5
8	Cariboo River - Upper
12	Chilko River - Chilko Lake to Bull Canyon (Chilcotin River)
14	Clearwater River
15	Cottonwood River - Upper and Middle
22	Fraser River - Upper: Red Pass to Mount Robson
23	Goat River - Milk River to Highway 16
24	Holmes River (Beaver River)
28	Morkill River (km 48 to Cushing Creek at km 37)
41	Quesnel River - Upper
47	Suskwa River
51	Torpy River - (Middle Canyon)
56	Willow River - Lower Lower

Park and Play Spots: park the car and go play! When you're done just stroll back to the vehicle.

6	Bowron River - Wayne's World
14	Clearwater River
33	Nautley River (at high water)
35	Nechako River - Walsh Wave and Whitemud Rapids
53	Wansa Creek Culvert

Alphabetical Index